A Screw Steamer at Neath c. 1848. Probably the *Neath Abbey*.

s.s. *NEATH ABBEY*

A BRISTOL CHANNEL COASTING STEAMER

Built at Neath Abbey 1846.
Wrecked at Nash Point 1894.

Allan Sutcliffe

Copyright © 2024 Allan Sutcliffe

All rights reserved. No part of this publication may be reproduced or transmitted in any form or by any means, electronic or mechanical including photocopying, recording or any information storage or retrieval system, without prior permission in writing from the publishers.

The right of Allan Sutcliffe to be identified as the author of this work has been asserted by him in accordance with the Copyright, Designs and Patents Act 1988

First published in the United Kingdom in 2024 by
The Choir Press

ISBN Paperback 978–1-78963–446–4
ISBN Hardback 978–1-78963–447–1

Contents

Foreword	ix
List of Illustrations	xi
Notes on the Spelling of Welsh Place Names, Currency and the Use of Italics	xiii
Acknowledgments	xiv
Sources	xv

CHAPTER 1
Neath Abbey Iron Works   1

CHAPTER 2
Marine Engineering and Shipbuilding at Neath Abbey   5

CHAPTER 3
The Screw Steamer *Neath Abbey*   11

CHAPTER 4
Navigation of the River Neath   19

CHAPTER 5
The *Neath Abbey*'s Working Life   23
   The Neath to Bristol Service   23
   Neath Abbey on the Somerset and Devon Coast   29
   Carmarthen to Bristol   34
   1886–1890   35
   Swansea to Bristol   36

CHAPTER 6
Passenger Traffic   39

CHAPTER 7
Excursions
Excursionists' Experiences and Local Reaction … 43

CHAPTER 8
Evan Evans's Personal Use of the *Neath Abbey* … 60

CHAPTER 9
Goods Traffic and the Coming of Railways … 63

CHAPTER 10
Thefts from Warehouses and the Ship … 70

CHAPTER 11
Accidents, Other Mishaps and Rescues … 73

CHAPTER 12
Crew … 80
    Masters … 81
    Mates … 85
    Engineers … 87
    Other Crew Members … 90

CHAPTER 13
Owners … 93

CHAPTER 14
Agents … 97

CHAPTER 15
Offices, Wharves and Warehouses … 99

CHAPTER 16
Disaster … 105

CHAPTER 17
Conclusion … 114

APPENDIX 1
Is the steamer in the painting by C. Hill the *Neath Abbey*?   116

APPENDIX 2
Joseph Lloyd Matthews (1834–1897) Agent at Neath
for the *Neath Abbey* 1859 to 1880   117

APPENDIX 3
A Note about R. H. Gunning   119

Endnotes   120

Foreword

As a schoolboy living in Neath in the late 1940s and early 1950s I often cycled to the nearby village of Neath Abbey and, after passing the remains of the Cistercian Abbey, wandered among the extensive ruined buildings between the Tennant Canal and the river. I also visited the silted-up dry dock. I knew little about these substantial remains of eighteenth and nineteenth century industry and believed that, apart from the dry dock, they had all been part of the Mines Royal Copper Works. It was only later that I learned that some of the ruined buildings were the remains of the Cheadle Copper Works that became the Marine Engineering premises of the Neath Abbey Iron Works.

These structures were demolished and buried when the A465 dual carriageway was built in the early 1970s. This was a major transport improvement but a great loss to the industrial archaeology of the area.

Shortly after returning to live in South Wales in late 2018 I bought a small poster or handbill, dating from 1870, advertising the Neath to Bristol shipping service operated by the steamer *Neath Abbey* which was built at the Neath Abbey Iron Works in 1846. This purchase led me into researching the history of the ship and its cross-channel service. I hoped to learn more about the ship, her working life, the men who sailed her, the owners and agents.

As well as being able to access the information held at public Archives and Records Offices, I have had the advantage of being able to search the vast number of newspaper pages made accessible online in recent years by the British Library and the National Library of Wales as well as information published on other websites. I have also benefited from the help of members of the Neath Antiquarian Society which has a substantial Archive.

Very little has been published previously about the *Neath Abbey* other than information about her dimensions and the circumstances of her destruction on the rocks at Nash Point in June 1894 with the loss of four lives. Not all of this published information is accurate.

The result of my efforts is this narrative in which I have attempted to demonstrate that the *Neath Abbey*, though not a big ship, represented an important step in the development of marine engineering and that by agreements for through carriage of goods, made with the railway companies that began to operate in South Wales from 1850 onwards, she played a part in progress towards an integrated transport system in the area. Where possible I have included information about people involved in her construction, ownership and operation. My account of excursion sailings by the *Neath Abbey* and other Bristol Channel steamers throws some light on leisure activities of South Wales work people.

The *Neath Abbey* was not unique and I believe that her history can be taken as representative of the very many steamships that traded on the Bristol Channel in the nineteenth century.

I hope that my account is a useful contribution to the history of the Neath area as well as to that of Bristol Channel coastal shipping.

I have tried to ensure the accuracy of my narrative but it is inevitable that I will have made some mistakes. For such errors I am entirely responsible.

List of Illustrations

Illustration 1   Frontispiece
A Screw Steamer at Neath c. 1848. Probably the *Neath Abbey*.
Detail from *The River Neath with the Ship 'Viola'* by C. Hill, c. 1848.
Neath Antiquarian Society.

Illustration 2   3
The Harbour of Neath 1846.
Section of *Map of Part of Swansea Bay*, by E. Moxham, 1846.
West Glamorgan Archive Service. WGAS D/D T 2371/1-2

Illustration 3   7
The Neath River from the Town Bridge to the Crown Copper Works.
From *Mr. Brereton's Report with Plan on the Floating of the River Neath*, 1872.
Neath Antiquarian Society Library.

Illustration 4   14
Evan Evans's High Street Brewery. Receipted Bill, 1846.
Author's Collection

Illustration 5   17
Builder's Certificate for the *Neath Abbey*, 1846.
West Glamorgan Archive Service. WGAS D/D PRO/SR/S/1846/1-7.

Illustration 6   32
Poster for Bristol, Neath, Ilfracombe and Bideford service, 1877.
Neath Antiquarian Society Aq-6-4-1

Illustration 7   67
Poster for Neath to Bristol Service December 1870
Author's Collection

Illustration 8 69
Letter from the *Neath Abbey* Agent 3 December 1870.
Author's Collection

Illustration 9 101
The Neath River from the Town Bridge to the Steam Packet Wharf, Neath
From *Mr. Brereton's Report with Plan on the Floating of the River Neath*, 1872.
Neath Antiquarian Society Library.

Illustration 10 104
Map of River Neath showing location of Steam Packet Wharf at Briton Ferry.
Part of *Plan of River Neath, showing Briton Ferry Docks, […] various named wharves*
Neath Antiquarian Society. NAS RE 13/8

Illustration 11 106
South Wales Echo 20 June 1894.
National Library of Wales.

Note on the Spelling of Welsh Place Names

Official documents, newspaper reports and other nineteenth century sources spelt Welsh place names in anglicised or corrupted ways that are no longer accepted. Thus, Llanelli is the standardised form of the name of the town previously referred to as Llanelly, and Hirwaun has replaced Hirwain. In quoting contemporary newspaper reports, advertisements, official names of companies or of other organisations or Acts of Parliament I have retained the spelling used. In my own text I have used today's standardised Welsh spelling. Thus I have referred to the steamship *Cambria* being built at Llanelli for the Llanelly Steam Navigation Company.

Note on Currency

In this account there are examples of prices and wages. They are quoted in the pre-decimal currency of the time in which there were twenty shillings in the pound, twelve pence in a shilling and two halfpennies or four farthings in a penny. Amounts were expressed as, for example, £1 5s. 6d., or 10¾d. or 4½d. An alternative method of expression was 15/6d. instead of 15s. 6d. Decimalisation in 1971 created a pound made up of 100 pence so a shilling became five pence and £1 5s. 0d. became £1.25. The farthing had ceased to be legal tender at the end of 1960.

   I have not made any attempt to convert the pre-decimal amounts into current equivalents after allowing for inflation because I do not think it is helpful. It is the relationship between prices and wages at the time that matters. However, for those interested £1 in 1850 is said to be equivalent to £168.71 in March 2024.[1]

Note on the use of italics

Italics used in advertisements and newspaper reports quoted have been retained. I have italicised all names of ships even when quoting from advertisements and reports in which names are not italicised.

Acknowledgments

The major sources of the information gathered in my research into the s.s. *Neath Abbey* are in two groups, original documents held in public archives and digitised newspapers available online.

The archivists and staff of the West Glamorgan Archive Service at Swansea and at the Bristol, Carmarthen and Gloucester Archives have provided a great deal of help. I am particularly grateful to Anne-Marie Gay at Swansea and Mary Milton at Bristol who have dealt with my enquiries patiently and courteously. Volunteers who run the Archives of the Neath Antiquarian Society have given me enthusiastic support, dealt with many questions and provided maps and other documents for me to see. David Michael, in particular, has dealt patiently with my questions, photographed the Neath Antiquarian Society items featured as illustrations, made suggestions and given valuable advice.

For access to newspapers I owe a great debt to the British Newspaper Archive of the British Library, the Welsh Newspapers Online website of the National Library of Wales and to Reach plc, a company that has the rights to a number of newspapers on those websites. Emyr Evans at the National Library of Wales and Natalie Jones of Reach plc were very helpful.

For my illustrations I am grateful to Kim Collis, the West Glamorgan County Archivist, for permission to use photographs of Moxham's Map and the ship's Builder's Certificate; the Committee of the Neath Antiquarian Society for permission to use photographs of part of the painting by C. Hill, Brereton's Map, the plan of Briton Ferry and the 1877 poster, and to the National Library of Wales for provision of and permission to use a photocopy of the heading of a report of the loss of the *Neath Abbey* in 1894. In addition, I have to thank my son-in-law and grandson, Jon and Adam Dix, for comments and the photographs of the three items from my collection.

I am also grateful to Bob Minty for information about the Harbour Commissioners and the Neath Port Authority.

Finally, I must express my gratitude to Rachel Woodman and Penelope Heal of Choir Press for all their patience and help in enabling this account to be published.

Sources

West Glamorgan Archives. (WGAS):
   Ship Registration Documents Transaction papers relating to the ship *Neath Abbey*   D/D PRO SR/S
   Crew Agreements and Lists   D/D PRO/CA

Bristol Archives
   Register of Ships, Second Series   37908/1/12
   Crew Lists   30182/538

Gloucester Record Office
   Crew List for the *Neath Abbey*, 1880   D3080/3948

Carmarthenshire Archives
   Index Card for *Neath Abbey*   HWLD 3948

The British Newspaper Archive   www.britishnewspaperarchive.co.uk

Welsh Newspapers   https://newspapers.library.wales/home

Reach plc   https://reachplc.com

Neath Antiquarian Society (NAS)   www.neathantiquariansociety.co.uk

https://ukcensusonline.com

Swansea Mariners.
   There are two databases:
      www.swanseamariners.org.uk/swanseamariners.php
         Merchant Seamen on Swansea Registered Ships. (This has information about crew of the *Neath Abbey* from 1865 to 1884 but there are many gaps.)
      www.swanseamariners.org.uk/registeredships.php
         Register of Swansea Shipping. Information about individual ships registered at Swansea.

E. Moxham, *Map of Part of Swansea Bay* [...] *Shewing the Harbours of Neath and Swansea* [...] by Egbert Moxham, Neath, Novr. 1846. WGAS D/D T 2371/1-2

R. P. Brereton, *Plan of Briton Ferry, showing River Neath, Briton Ferry docks, […] various named wharves, Giants Grave Pill and Court Sart Pill*, by Alfred Williams, Great George Street, Westminster, London; n.d. (c. 1860?) NAS RE 13/8

Laurence Ince, *Neath Abbey and the Industrial Revolution* (Tempus Publishing, 2001).

Keith Tucker, A *Scratch in Glamorganshire*, (Historical Projects, 1998).

D. Rhys Phillips, *The History of the Vale of Neath*, (Published by the Author, Swansea, 1925.)

Grahame Farr, *West Country Passenger Services*, 2nd Edition, (T. Stephenson & Sons, Ltd., 1967.)

Stephen R. Fox, *Transatlantic: Samuel Cunard, Isambard Brunel, and the Great Atlantic Steamships*. (Harper Collins, 2003).

Trevor Boyns and Colin Baber, 'The Supply of Labour 1750 – 1914,' in Arthur H. John & Glanmor Williams (eds.) *The Glamorgan County History*, Vol. V. *Industrial Glamorgan*, Chapter VII, 322–323.

G. A. Taylor, *Transactions of the Neath Antiquarian Society*, 1937/1939, quoted in Cliff Morgan, *Briton Ferry Notes*, (Briton Ferry Y.M.C.A., n. d.), 5.

Harry Green, 'Ships of Old Neath, Neath Abbey and Briton Ferry', *Transactions of the Neath Antiquarian Society 1980–81*, 110.

John Morris, 'Evan Evans and the Vale of Neath Brewery,' in *Morgannwg, Transactions of the Glamorgan Local History Society*, Vol. IX, 1965, 38–60.

Martin Phillips, *The Copper Industry in the Port Talbot District*, (The Guardian Press, Neath, 1935), 63–64.

Charles E. Lee, *The Swansea and Mumbles Railway*, 2nd Edition (Oakwood Press, 1954).

D. S. M. Barrie, *A Regional History of the Railways of Great Britain, Volume XII, South Wales*. 2nd Edition (David St John Thomas, 1994).

CHAPTER 1

Neath Abbey Iron Works

The town of Neath, a few miles east of Swansea, is located on the tidal River Neath at the lowest point at which in early times it was relatively safe and easy to cross. A lower crossing point for the main road through South Wales was not created until a bridge was built at Briton Ferry and opened in 1955. The Roman road through South Wales, the Via Julia Maritima, crossed the river close to present day Neath and the Romans established a fort, Nidum, on the west bank a little below the present town. The Normans recognised the importance of this crossing point and built a castle, first on the west bank and then later on the east bank where its ruined successor still stands. A town grew up close to this castle and fairs and a market developed. In 1130 an Abbey was established on land outside the town on the west bank of the river. The Cistercian Neath Abbey became important and prosperous until it was dissolved by Henry VIII in 1539. Shortly before the dissolution John Leland, 'the King's Antiquary', described it as 'the fairest abbey of all Wales'.[2]

By the last decade of the eighteenth-century Neath had become an important commercial and industrial centre. With some difficulty the tidal river was navigable for seagoing ships up to the bridge in the town and boats small enough to pass under it could go a little further up to Aberdulais. The South Wales Coalfield extends to the sea in this western part of the old county of Glamorgan providing considerable advantage in the cost of transport to ports and making an abundant supply of coal available for industrial development on the coast. Copper smelting and iron making developed.

Although the old-established copper works at Melincryddan on the left bank of the River Neath below the town closed in about 1796, on the opposite side of the river, also below the town, there were three copper works near the ruins of the medieval Abbey. The works of Roe and Company, later known as the Cheadle Copper Works, and the Mines Royal Copper Works, were both close to the ruins on the right bank of the River Clydach just above its confluence with the Neath. About half a mile downstream of that point were the Crown Copper Works. Along the Neath Valley there were also a number of iron works for which power was provided by waterfalls on tributaries of the river Neath close to the points at which they flowed into the main river. One of these was a small iron works on the River Clydach, approximately a quarter of a mile above the ruins of the medieval Abbey.[3]

A very important transport development was the authorisation of the Neath Canal in 1791 and its opening in stages in 1793 and 1795. The canal ran down the Neath Valley from Glynneath to Melincryddan, just south of the town. It was extended to Giant's Grave at Briton Ferry in 1799. This canal provided improved transport of coal to the sea, and of raw materials and products between the works in the Valley and the coast.[4]

In 1800 legislation established the Neath Harbour Commissioners responsible for licensing pilots and hobblers and for regulating their numbers and duties. The Commissioners' numbers and powers were increased substantially by the Neath Harbour Act of 1843 when they were given full responsibility for the administration of Neath Harbour extending from just above the bridge in the town of Neath to Swansea Bay.[5]

Much of the copper ore smelted at Neath Abbey came from Cornwall. One of the Cornish businesses involved was a partnership consisting mainly of members of the Fox, Tregelles and Price families with interests in copper ore, tin smelting and iron. They were Quakers. In 1792 this Cornish partnership leased the small iron works at Neath Abbey and enlarged them. Two very large masonry blast furnaces, one 65 ft high and the other 53 ft were built in 1793. Machine shops were enlarged and other workshops including a forge and rolling mill were built.

The ships of the partnership brought copper ore to be smelted at Neath Abbey and returned to Perran Wharf, their base near Falmouth where they had an iron foundry, carrying iron ore from the Vale of Neath, coal from mines near Neath Abbey and products of their Neath Abbey Iron Works.

In 1818 the name of the business was changed from Messrs. Foxes and Neath Abbey Iron Company to The Neath Abbey Iron Company. From making pig iron, iron plates, cylinders, pipes, pumps and parts for steam engines, the Neath Abbey business began manufacturing and selling complete beam engines that were regarded as expensive but well-made and reliable.

At first many of their engines went to Cornish mines for pumping and winding but as the South Wales coal and iron industries developed the partnership concentrated more on meeting the demands of those industries.

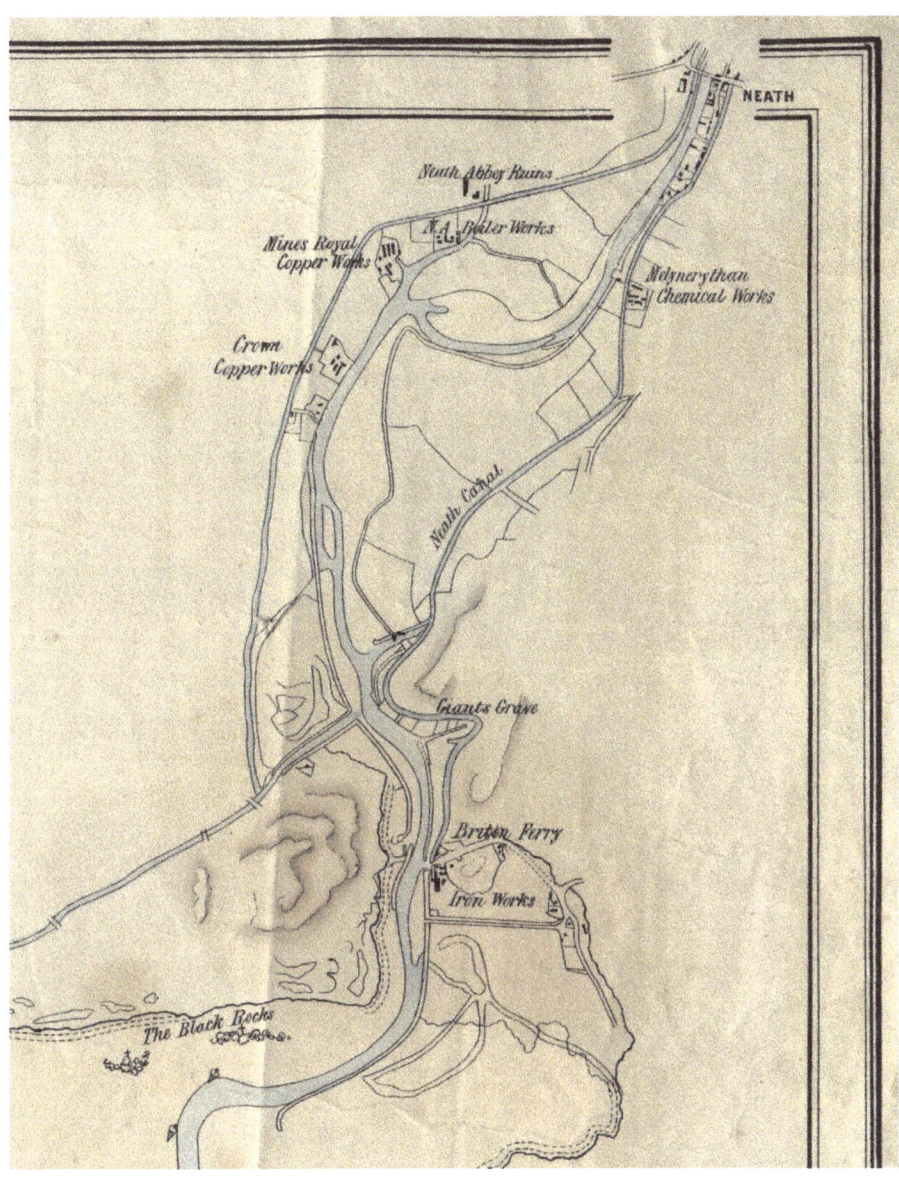

Illustration 2
The Harbour of Neath 1846.

In addition, they exported engines all over the world. Their range of engines was extended to include table engines, grasshopper beam engines, horizontal stationary engines and marine engines. From 1829 they were building railway engines. Thus the Neath Abbey Iron Works built every sort of steam engine as well as a wide range of other iron products, including structural iron work, mill work, weighing machines, sawing machines, small aqueducts and gas making plant.

Two men were mainly responsible for expanding the Neath Abbey Iron Works, diversifying the range of products and developing the reputation of the company. Peter Price was managing partner of the Iron Works from 1801 until 1818 when he was succeeded by his son, Joseph Tregelles Price, who managed the works until his death on Christmas Day, 1854.[6]

The Tennant Canal, built by George Tennant of Cadoxton Lodge, Neath, opened in 1824, connecting Swansea to the Neath Canal at Aberdulais just above Neath, thus enabling coal and other products to be shipped from the Vale of Neath to Swansea instead of continuing down the Neath Canal to Briton Ferry.[7] The Tennant Canal passes between the site of the Cheadle Works and the ruined Abbey. In about 1828 two short branch canals were constructed at Neath Abbey, one towards the main Iron Works, and the other in the opposite direction into the Cheadle Works.[8] Using the Neath and the Tennant canals iron ore and anthracite could be shipped from the company's mines at Abernant, near Glynneath, to Neath Abbey. Later, when iron making was concentrated at the Abernant works, pig iron could be shipped instead of iron ore.[9]

CHAPTER 2

Marine Engineering and Shipbuilding at Neath Abbey

Before the end of 1816 the paddle steamer *Britannia*, built at Greenock in that year for the Dublin to Holyhead passenger service, came to Neath Abbey for alterations to her 20 horsepower engines made by James Cook of Glasgow. Ince states that the *Britannia* 'was heading for Bristol when it was found necessary to put into Neath Abbey'.[10] In fact this work was pre-planned. In December 1816 *The Cambrian* reported that the owners of the *Britannia*, having:

> found that their machinery, although the best then known, and admirably adapted to a river, was incapable of contending to advantage with a heavy sea, it therefore became necessary to make alterations; and as Mr. Alexander Nimmo and Mr. Henry H. Price, in the course of their investigation of the subject, had discovered some valuable improvements, they were employed to introduce them and are now, we understand, engaged at the Engine Manufactory of Messrs. Foxes and Neath Abbey Iron Co. in carrying them into effect on the *Britannia* steam packet. We learn that in three or four weeks she will be ready for sea, when the public will be gratified by seeing her manoeuvre in the Swansea Bay and Bristol Channel.[11]

When this work was completed the *Britannia* steamed to Bristol, arriving on 29 April 1817, 'making the passage against the ebb tide in twelve hours'.[12]

Alexander Nimmo (1783–1832) was a Scottish civil engineer who worked in Ireland from 1811 mapping bogs, preparing navigation charts of Ireland's coasts, designing and altering harbours, carrying out river improvements and other civil engineering work.[13] Henry H. Price was Henry Habberly Price (1794–c.1839), a brother of Joseph Tregelles Price. He was a civil engineer, with a great interest in locomotives and marine engines, and made a substantial contribution to the development of the Neath Abbey Iron Works. He had worked on river improvement in Ireland and quite probably worked for Nimmo. On 18 March 1823 Price was granted a patent 'for an apparatus for giving increased effect to paddles used in steam vessels, applicable to rotary movements, by which they are generally worked'.[14]

The work on the *Britannia* is the earliest evidence of interest in marine engineering at the Neath Abbey Iron Works. While she was at Neath Abbey the Company's engineers made detailed drawings of the ship's engines and it appears that the company set about collecting information concerning steam propulsion. For this purpose 'Neath Abbey engineers were sent to examine and report on the engines of various vessels. Indeed the Neath Abbey Iron Works collection in the West Glamorgan Archives contains reports sent back from Dover in January and February 1822 concerning the machinery of the paddle steamer *Arrow*'.[15]

The development of that interest into a successful marine engineering business reached an important stage in 1822 when Neath Abbey marine engines were fitted to the wooden paddle steamer *Glamorgan* which had been built at Rotherhithe on the River Thames.[16] She began a regular Swansea to Bristol service on 12 April 1823. The advertisement for the service stated that it was 'calculated that the average passage will not exceed nine hours'.[17]

Ince lists seven other ships fitted with engines at Neath Abbey in the period before 1842, five paddle steamers built at Bristol, one paddle steamer built at Newport and the wooden paddle tug *Dragon Fly* built by Allen & Luly [*sic*] at Neath in 1840 and referred to in more detail in Chapter 15.

To meet the needs of this business, in 1824 the company took over the vacant premises of the Cheadle Copper Works and converted them for building marine engines and boilers.[18] The location was ideal for fitting engines to ships built elsewhere and for ship building, situated on the Clydach River with its own wharf just above its confluence with the River Neath. This works was known locally as '*y gwaith bach*,' the little works, to distinguish it from the main works a little higher up the Clydach.[19] Also it was only a short distance on the level from the main works and in due course the two sites were connected by a tramroad that ran past the West Front of the Abbey.[20]

The Company's marine engineering business was extended to include shipbuilding and in 1842 it built its first ship, the paddle steamer *Prince of Wales*, the first iron ship built in Wales. She was launched on the morning of 25 February:

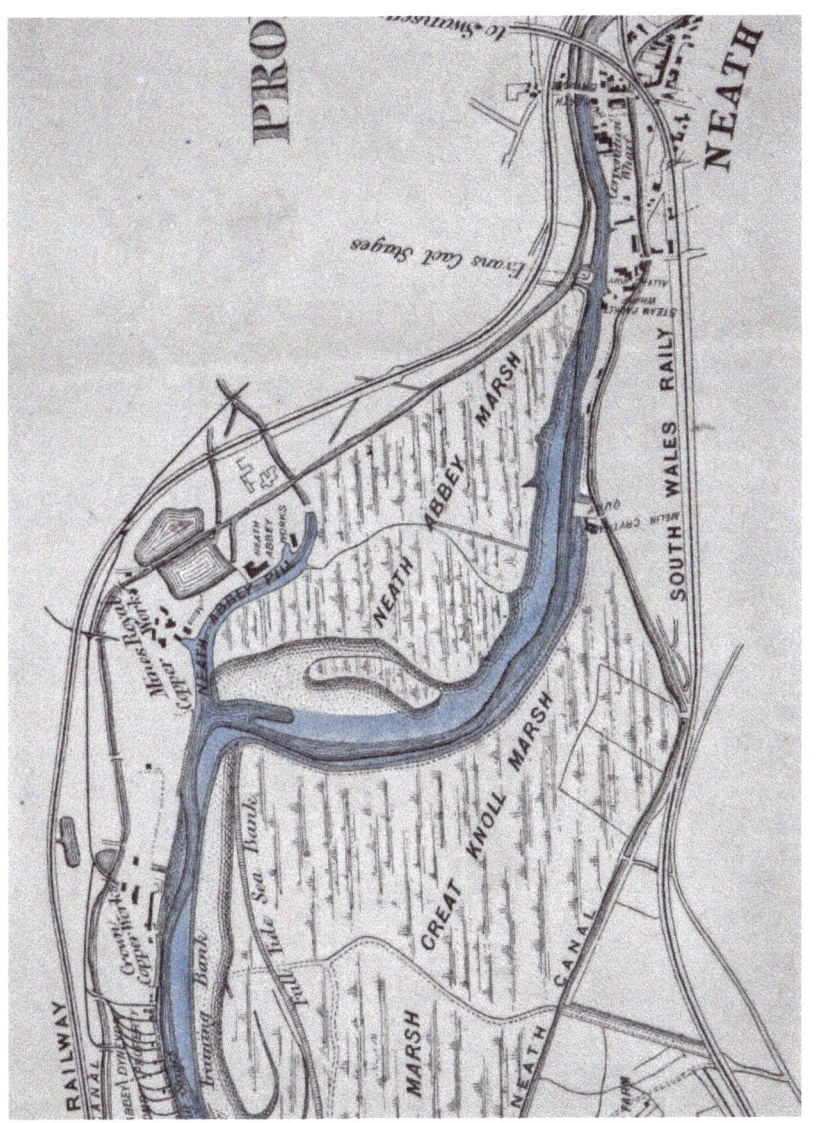

Illustration 3
The Neath River from the Town Bridge to the Crown Copper Works.

[…] when she went off the stocks in beautiful style. She is formed in the strongest manner, is divided into three compartments by two watertight iron bulkheads, on the late approved plan. Her model has been much admired by many good judges. In consideration of this being the first Iron Steamer built by the Neath Abbey Iron Co., about 250 of the workmen employed in the factory were provided with a substantial breakfast on the occasion.[21]

The *Prince of Wales* was 120 ft. long, 182 tons gross, 106 tons nett with two 32 in. engines. She commenced sailing on the Cardiff to Bristol route during the week ended 30 April 1842.[22]

A paddle tug, the *Pioneer*, was launched on 7 October 1842.[23]

The company's first screw-propelled steamer, the *Henry Southan*, 103.6ft, long, 117 tons gross, 78 tons nett, with two 28in. engines,[24] and intended for carrying goods and passengers between Gloucester and Swansea, was launched from a 'patent slip' on the evening of 21 July 1845, 'amid the enthusiastic cheering of the assembled thousands'.[25]

The Neath Abbey Iron Company was innovative in building iron ships when there was still some scepticism about the suitability of iron for shipbuilding. They were even more adventurous in adopting screw propulsion when there was considerable doubt about its suitability for ocean-going ships.

Although shipbuilders such as William Fairbairn and John Laird were building iron ships by 1840 there were still many who doubted the suitability of iron. There were concerns about matters such as the quality of iron plates, the rigidity of iron ships, rust and corrosion, the inability to sheath the hull in copper to prevent fouling and also iron hulls created their own magnetic fields causing compass deviations.[26] John Grantham, a prominent naval architect and consulting engineer and authority on the use of iron in shipbuilding, was consulted by Brunel in 1838 about the best iron plates and braces for marine purposes.[27] In a contribution to the Philosophical Society of Liverpool in 1842, Grantham, President of the Society, commented:

> Many, therefore, still view the subject [iron shipbuilding] with distrust and regard it as one of the visionary schemes of this wonder working age which will soon be relinquished and forgotten.[28]

The adoption of screw propulsion was even more adventurous. Paddle wheels driven by steam power were well-established and acceptable even though their inefficiency was recognised. A number of people had designed screw propellers, but none had been successful until in May 1836 F. P. Smith patented a design for a steam vessel powered by a screw at the stern. He gained financial support, and a small screw steamer was built. This led to the launch of a larger vessel on the Thames in 1838. She was the *Archimedes*, the world's first successful screw-propelled steamship.[29]

After completing a tour around Britain in 1840 the *Archimedes* was lent to Isambard Kingdom Brunel for tests while the *Great Britain* was being built. Brunel was critical of the *Archimedes* itself, considering the engine and gearing as faulty, the vessel badly designed and the levels of noise and vibration too high for passengers. However, he concluded that:

> With proper design and engineering the screw offered compelling advantages. It would save weight especially at the top of the vessel, where high paddle wheels and their machinery raised a vessel's center of gravity, and made her less stable in heavy seas. It allowed for a simple more compact ship structure, with more space below for cargo and passengers. By eliminating the bulky paddle boxes, it offered less resistance to head winds and waves. When a ship rolled from side to side, a screw would remain submerged and moving the ship forward, unlike side paddle wheels which could roll out of the water, alternately racing and overloading the engine, harming machinery. Without paddle boxes a ship would present less beam for tight maneuvers in rivers and harbors. Paddles might start a voyage too deeply immersed under a full load of coal, and then rise too far out of the water as fuel was burned; a screw stayed efficiently under water regardless. Screw machinery cost less initially and – because it was less vulnerable to passing shocks – would be cheaper and less trouble to maintain.[30]

As the result of these tests with the *Archimedes* and although the *Great Britain* was already partly built with provision for paddle wheel engines, the design of the ship was altered to provide for screw propulsion in place of paddle wheels.

In spite of Brunel's adoption of the screw propeller great scepticism about the suitability of screw propulsion for ocean-going ships persisted. This is demonstrated by a comment in the first issue of the journal *Scientific American*, publication of which coincided with the *Great Britain*'s arrival in New York in August 1845 at the end of her first transatlantic voyage. Reporting on this event *The Scientific American* stated:

> If there is anything objectionable in the construction or machinery of this noble ship, it is the mode of propelling her by the screw propeller;

and we should not be surprised if it should be, ere long, superseded by paddle wheels at the sides.[31]

Thus, by adopting screw propulsion for the *Henry Southan* in 1845, the Neath Abbey Iron Company was at the forefront of steamship development at a time when substantial doubt about screw propulsion remained in the marine engineering world.

It should be noted that the Neath Abbey Iron Works dry dock was not constructed until 1853.[32] Until then ships built at the Works were launched from a slipway on the river bank.

CHAPTER 3

The Screw Steamer *Neath Abbey*

The Neath Abbey Iron Company's fourth ship, the *Neath Abbey*, screw-propelled like the *Henry Southan* but a little smaller, was launched at Neath Abbey on 10 June 1846, as described in the following two reports.

On Wednesday evening last, a very beautiful iron steamer was launched from the patent slip of the Neath Abbey Iron Company, built by Mr. T. Clement, under the able superintendence of A. Sturge, Esq., for a company of shareholders, the whole of whom are merchants and tradesmen of the town of Neath, who feeling the necessity of a more rapid communication between that port and Bristol, for the conveyance of goods and passengers, and of obviating not only the inconvenience but the great expense of a combination of freight, heavy dues and land carriage consequent upon receiving goods *via* Swansea, have determined upon effecting this most desirable object. The steamer is named very appropriately the *Neath Abbey* [and] is very much admired, and reflects great credit upon all parties engaged in her construction. Her engines are of 60-horse power with patent condensers and screw propeller, and are also manufactured by the celebrated Neath Abbey Iron Company. She will be ready for the station in about 3 weeks, when her first trip will be to Tenby, taking with her the shareholders and their friends on a pleasure excursion. (*The Welshman*)[33]

On Wednesday se'nnight, was launched from the building yard of the Neath Abbey Company, an iron steamer, called the *Neath Abbey*, which is to be propelled by the screw. She glided from the ways in good style, amidst the cheering of a large number of spectators from Neath and elsewhere. She is nearly 100 feet in length, and is to be fitted with a pair of sixty-horse power condensing engines, connected directly to the propeller shaft. Her bow is remarkably fine, and her appearance both on the stocks and in the water excited general admiration. The deck is flush, and the cabins, contrary to the usual practice, are placed nearly in the centre of the vessel. They are to be handsomely fitted up with panels containing views of the various and beautiful scenery of the neighbourhood, painted by Mr. Butler, of Swansea. Her proprietors are a joint stock company, composed mainly of the respectable tradesmen of Neath. The vessel is to be run between that town and Bristol. (*The Cambrian*)[34]

The *Cambrian* was mistaken in describing the ship as having a pair of 60 horse power engines. That was her total horse power.

Alfred Sturge was the son of a Gloucester merchant, Thomas Sturge. The 1841 Census lists Alfred Sturge, aged 15 [*sic*], not born in the Neath Registration District, living at James Street, Neath, with the occupation of engineer. As a draughtsman at Neath Abbey Iron Works he was credited with the design of other ships built there: the *Henry Southan* in 1845[35] and the *La Serena* in 1848.[36] In that year he became managing partner of the Swansea Iron Shipbuilding Company.[37] One of the few ships built by that company was the *Fire Fly* which was fitted with engines at Neath Abbey in 1849.[38]

Thomas Clement was born at Melincryddan, Neath, in about 1780. An announcement of the marriage of his daughter Mary to David Evans, son of John Evans, engineer, Neath Abbey Works, at Cadoxton Church, Neath, on 17 October 1850, describes him as 'iron ship-builder and boiler maker'.[39] In 1851 the Census listed Thomas Clement, widower, aged 71, boiler maker, living at Neath Abbey with his son in law, David Evans, engine fitter, and his daughter, Mary. He was probably the Thomas Clement, 'artisan,' who in May 1852 bought one of the sixty-four shares in the *Dragon Fly*.[40]

Although Alfred Sturge and Thomas Clement are credited with building the *Neath Abbey*, the Builder named in the 1846 Registration documents was Nathaniel Tregelles.[41] He was a relative of Joseph Tregelles Price and a partner in the Iron Works Company and must have had overall responsibility for the building of the ship.

With admirable foresight *The Cambrian* also commented that the *Neath Abbey*'s:

> small size and compact form for the cargo she is to carry (60 tons) have caused surprise. This is one of the great advantages which the use of the screw propeller affords: the draught of water of a paddle steamer cannot

vary much without injuring the action of the paddles, whilst the efficiency of the screw is invariably increased by greater immersion, so that with the latter a vessel of much less size may be used, whereby the first cost is diminished materially. This fact, when generally known, will no doubt lead to a much more extended adoption of the principle of screw propulsion than has hitherto been the case.

So *The Cambrian*, published in Swansea, recognised the importance of screw propulsion for the future development of steamships while *The Scientific American* had failed to do so.

The 'respectable tradesmen of Neath' were Evan Evans, Jonathan Rees and Paul Evans French. They were co-partners holding the 64 shares jointly. In 1846 Evan Evans was trading as a brewer, owning the High Street Brewery in Neath (see Illustration 4, page 14). Paul Evans French was a druggist carrying on business in New Street, Neath. He died at Neath on 10 May 1847, 'highly and deservedly respected, aged 28'.[42] Jonathan Rees was a member of a prominent Quaker family in Neath where his father, Evan Rees, had established a business as an ironmonger in 1770–1773. He died in 1869.[43]

Unfortunately, there is no illustration that can be identified with certainty as being of the *Neath Abbey*. However, a ship in the river below Neath river bridge shown in a painting by C. Hill, c.1848, in the collection of the Neath Antiquarian Society, has been described as 'possibly the *Neath Abbey* […] or equally likely the *Henry Southan* […] and possibly neither ship'.[44] The original painting shows four ships in the river at Neath with the bridge in the background. Three of these are sailing ships. The other is clearly a screw steamer, having a tall funnel, two masts and no paddle wheels. She is close to a stone-built quay with a crane and a warehouse. (The entire painting is shown on the Art UK website.[45]) I believe that the probability that the painting represents the *Neath Abbey* is very high indeed. My reasons for this opinion are set out in Appendix 1. Whether she is the *Neath Abbey* or not the painting may be regarded as a good representation of a ship very much like her.

Further information about the ship was given by Joseph Tregelles Price himself in a speech at the meeting of The British Association for the Advancement of Science held at Swansea in August 1848, when he commented on an address by Mr. J. Scott Russell entitled *Progress of Steam Ship Building*.

> Mr. J. Price rose to say that he agreed with Mr. Russell in all he had adduced. There was, however, one mode of steam navigation – one

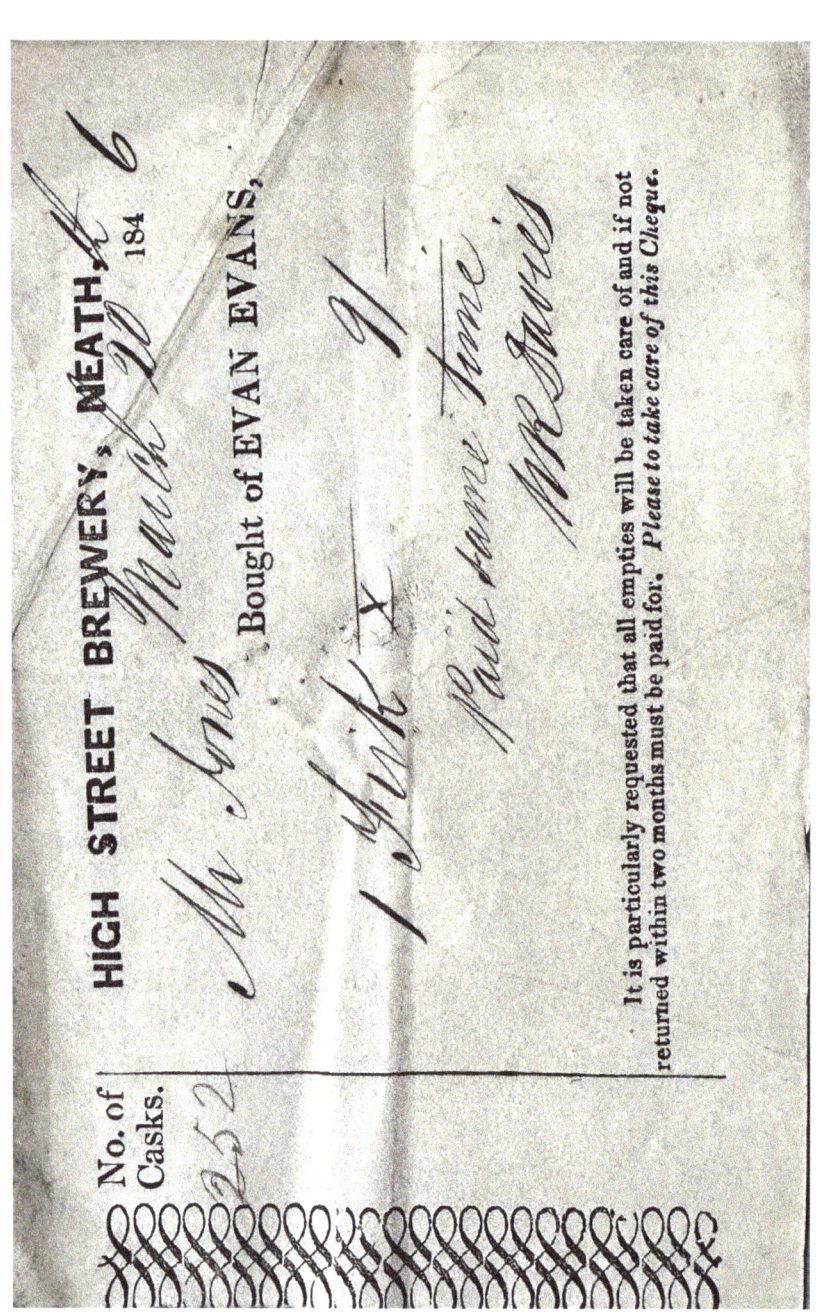

Illustration 4
Evan Evans's High Street Brewery. Receipted Bill, 1846.

mode of propulsion to which he had not alluded; he meant the mode of propulsion by the screw propeller. He would, therefore, mention that they had built a little vessel called the *Neath Abbey*, which plied from Neath to Bristol, a distance of upwards of sixty miles, and which had only two 12-inch cylinders, in fact a mere toy, of course using high steam [*sic*]. Now she could walk round the *Beresford*, which had two 40 horse-power engines: the working her upon the high-pressure principle necessarily increased the speed of the piston. With these engines they had stepped out of the old track. They had not adopted the American plan of puffing off the steam, but of a high-pressure engine without puffing off the steam and without using a jet of cold water. He confessed that when this plan was proposed by his younger coadjutors, he, as one of the old fashioned, hesitated – but at length he consented. The *Neath Abbey* had a screw propeller with three blades, which were immersed under the water – her propeller being about 3½ feet in diameter. The vessel is built in the best form, allowing sufficient breadth for her engines. The two 12-inch cylinders are placed diagonally, and slung up by wrought iron beams; and they lay hold of one crank pin like the hands of two men working at a grindstone; and thus they conducted [*sic*] their engines almost in a snuff-box. Then they employed their boiler in the manner described by Mr. Russell. Then they came to the condensation of the steam, which they did not allow to go puffing off, but let it pass back into the boiler condensed, and in a distilled state, which accounted for their never having any mud or dirt in their boilers.[46]

The method by which steam was condensed was described in more detail by J. T. Price in a contribution to the Meeting of the British Association in 1851 entitled *On a Method of condensing Steam in Marine Engines, at present employed in several Steam Vessels in the Bristol Channel.*[47]

John Scott Russell was an eminent naval architect, ship builder and civil engineer who collaborated with Brunel in building the *Great Eastern*. The fact that in his Address Russell had mentioned boiler improvements and commented on paddles but did not comment on screw propulsion suggests that in 1848 he was not convinced of the advantages of this new method of propulsion.

When first registered at the Swansea Registry in 1846 with the Port Number of 17/1846 the length of the *Neath Abbey* was 97ft, her breadth amidships 16.4ft, depth in hold at midships 9ft, and the length of the Engine

Room, which occupied the full breadth of the ship, was 20ft. The Registered Tonnage was 67. She was clench built of iron, with a round stern, two masts schooner rigged, one deck, no gallery, no figurehead, and with a standing bowsprit[48] (see Illustration 5, page 17). It should be noted that on Registration documents measurements were expressed to tenths of a foot, not in feet and inches. On 1 June 1855 she was given the Official Number 3948.[49] Clench, or clinker, built means that the iron plates of her hull overlapped. Schooner rigged indicates that she had fore and aft sails and the foremast was shorter than the main mast.

From mid-May until mid-October 1865 the *Neath Abbey* did not sail. She underwent 'thorough repair and enlargement' at Neath Abbey. This required re-registration at Swansea. The Certificate of Survey dated 12 October gives her length as 109.6ft, her main breadth as 17.1ft and the length of the engine room as 19.1ft. This greater length was not the result of a difference in the way the ship was measured. The Certificate is endorsed by the Measuring Surveyor with the words, 'This vessel was lengthened by 10 feet'.[50]

When first registered in 1846 she was described as having no figurehead but in the action for damages brought against the owners in 1886 by the Conservators of the River Avon, for causing damage to a crane barge in the River Avon, described in Chapter 11, it was reported that 'some of the scroll work near the figurehead was damaged'. It is reasonable to assume that the figurehead was fitted as part of this work of enlargement especially as the report of her first voyage after completion of the work referred to her 'new face.'[51]

The ship was re-registered again in 1871 and the length of the engine room was shown as 10ft.[52] Given the measurements in previous documents this clearly raised a question. A letter from the Tonnage Department dated 2 January 1871 confirmed the measurement.[53] Some internal rearrangement must have been made.

The calculation of the Registered Tonnage of a ship was based on the measurement of the total volume of enclosed spaces converted to tons at the rate of 100 cu. ft. equalling one ton. In 1874 the Tonnage Deck space, the space below the single deck, amounted to 97.16 tons and the enclosed space above the Tonnage Deck, the 'Break', was 16.03 giving the Gross Tonnage of 113.19. From this total it was necessary to deduct the tonnage equivalent of 'space required for propelling power,' 36.22 tons and 'space occupied by Seamen [...] and kept free from Goods or Stores,' 10.86 tons, a total deduction of 47.08 tons. The net effect was the Registered Tonnage in 1874 of 66.11.[54] The composition of the Space occupied by Seamen was detailed in

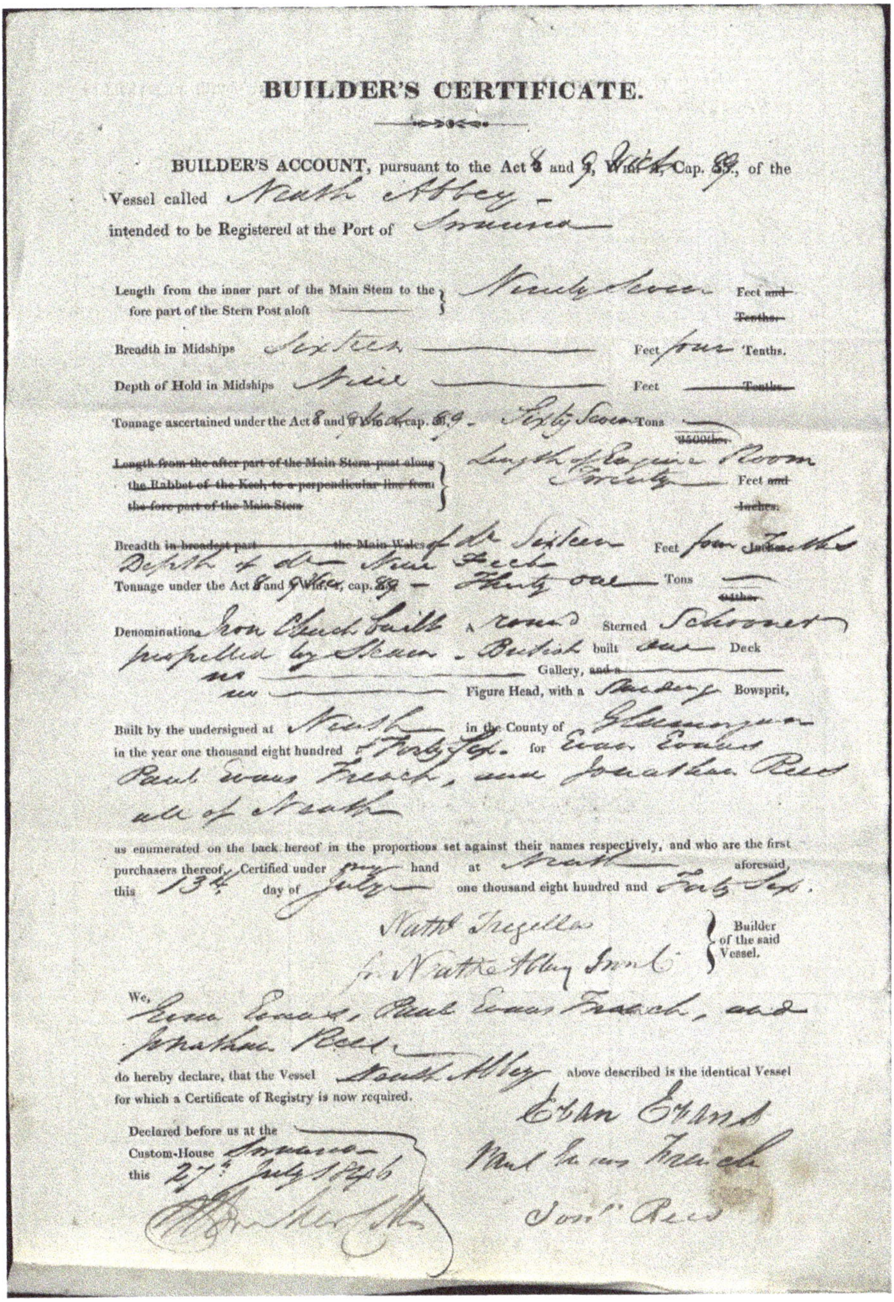

BUILDER'S CERTIFICATE.

BUILDER'S ACCOUNT, pursuant to the Act 8 and 9, Vict., Cap. 89, of the Vessel called Neath Abbey — intended to be Registered at the Port of Swansea —

Length from the inner part of the Main Stem to the fore part of the Stern Post aloft — Ninety seven — Feet ~~and Tenths~~.

Breadth in Midships Sixteen — Feet four Tenths.

Depth of Hold in Midships Nine — Feet ~~Tenths~~

Tonnage ascertained under the Act 8 and 9 Vict. cap. 89 — Sixty Seven Tons ~~3500ths~~

~~Length from the after part of the Main Stern-post along the Rabbet of the Keel, to a perpendicular line from the fore part of the Main Stem~~ Length of Engine Room Twenty — Feet ~~and Inches~~

Breadth ~~in broadest part — the Main Wales~~ of do Sixteen Feet four ~~Inches~~ Tenths

Depth of do Nine Feet

Tonnage under the Act 8 and 9 Vict., cap. 89 — Thirty one — Tons ~~ths~~

Denomination Iron Clinch built a round Sterned Schooner propelled by Steam — British built one Deck no Gallery, ~~and a~~ no Figure Head, with a Standing Bowsprit,

Built by the undersigned at Neath in the County of Glamorgan in the year one thousand eight hundred & Forty Six. for Evan Evans Paul Evans French, and Jonathan Rees all of Neath

as enumerated on the back hereof in the proportions set against their names respectively, and who are the first purchasers thereof, Certified under my hand at Neath aforesaid, this 13th day of July one thousand eight hundred and Forty Six.

Nathl Tregelles for Neath Abbey Iron Co — Builder of the said Vessel.

We, Evan Evans, Paul Evans French, and Jonathan Rees do hereby declare, that the Vessel Neath Abbey above described is the identical Vessel for which a Certificate of Registry is now required.

Evan Evans
Paul Evans French
Jona. Rees

Declared before us at the Custom-House Swansea this 27th July 1846

Illustration 5
Builder's Certificate for the *Neath Abbey*, 1846.

the 'Surveyor's Report on Crew Space' in December 1870 and shows that space occupied by Seamen in the Lower Forecastle accommodated four men representing a tonnage deduction of 4.86 and Mates and Engineers' Berths in an unspecified part of the ship accommodated 6 men representing a deduction of 6.0 tons.[55]

This tonnage information was repeated in the Bristol Register of Ships when she was registered there in 1886 but was amended in 1891 by the insertion of a further deduction in the calculation of Registered Tonnage of 4.40 tons in accordance with the Merchant Shipping (Tonnage) Act, 1889. This was made up of the Master's Berth, 2.95 tons, and the Bosun's Store, 1.45 tons. The effect was to reduce the Registered Tonnage to 61.71.[56] In subsequent official documents this tonnage was given variously as 60, 61 or 62.

In 1875 'extensive Cabin alterations and improvements' were carried out. The work was probably done at Bristol where she was based at that time. The work included the fitting of a new steam-winch and was done preparatory to beginning to call 'early in October (in connection with her Bideford trade) at Ilfracombe Quay, with and for passengers and goods'.[57]

In 1848 Joseph Tregelles Price had said that the ship had two 12in. cylinders. However, in 1886 Mary Bevan, the daughter of Evan Evans, informed the Swansea Registry that she was the owner of the ship following the death of her father in 1871 and for this purpose had to make a 'Declaration by Representative of a Deceased Owner taking by Transmission'. In this it was stated that the *Neath Abbey* had two 13in. cylinders with an 18in. length of Stroke.[58]

CHAPTER 4

Navigation of the River Neath

Between her launch in June 1846, and November 1887 when sailings were suspended because of the financial difficulties of her owners, the *Neath Abbey* probably sailed over the bar and into the River Neath more than 3,500 times. Therefore some comments on the River seem appropriate.

The town of Neath is 3¼ miles upriver from the sea[59] and the river has always presented some navigational difficulties. The entrance to the river between Crymlyn Burrows on the northwest, Swansea side, and Witford Point on the southeast, Port Talbot side, was described in 1839 as:

> nearly half a mile wide from shore to shore, but the channel is narrow and intricate, having high sand-banks on the Witford side, and on the other the Black Rocks in front of the Burrows; besides which the low-water flat of sand, called Neath Bar, dries out in a S. W. direction 2¾ miles, though variously guttered by the freshes which fret their way down to low water-mark. The deepest of these approaches to the river carries 17 feet water on springs and 11 feet on neaps, and is marked by 3 black can-buoys, which are succeeded by perches on the Black Rocks. [...] The outer can-buoy lies almost a mile within the low water-mark, and bears from the Mumbles Lighthouse E. by N. 4 miles. Nothing should tempt a vessel bound to Neath to pass that buoy without a pilot, even supposing the weather such that none can board her; she had better wait under the Mumbles till it moderates; for, were she to cross the bar safely, the intricacy of the channel and the furious tide near Briton Ferry would so perplex any stranger that he would lose all command of his vessel; yet with the aid of pilots the trade of this port is carried on with very few accidents.[60]

This description was repeated as late as 1867.[61]

In December 1869 'A Merchant' wrote a letter to the editor of the *Shipping & Mercantile Gazette* in which he explained that he was 'largely interested in the Trade of Neath, and having a knowledge of its immense mineral resources, together with a stake therein, [and had] a more than ordinary anxiety for the advancement and improvement of the Port and Harbour. Hence I am desirous to bring before your numerous readers the advantages which the Port possesses, convinced that many of them are totally unaware of the great changes and improvements which have recently been made both in the Port and River entrance thereto.' He went on to quote from the 1867 edition of *Sailing Directions for the Bristol Channel* which had exactly the same description as the 1837 edition commenting that 'this description would be enough to deter any Shipowner from sending a vessel of any size to the Port, and make the Britonferry [*sic*] Docks [...] practically useless.' He then contrasted that with the 1869 edition.

> This entrance is now a straight channel, in a N.E. by E. ¾E. direction. The embankment which has been constructed, leading to Britonferry and the River beyond, is marked by red perches on the right and by black buoys on the left, and at springs a vessel may carry 25 feet over it at high water, and 17 at neaps.

He ended his letter:

> Now it will be manifest from the foregoing that the quiet perseverance of the Harbour Commissioners has brought about a vastly improved state of things, and that they have converted a tortuous channel with 17 feet of water through fretted gutters into a straight one entirely out to sea with a depth of 25 feet.

> Having been connected with Shipping, and possessing some knowledge of Navigation, I may assert that nothing is now easier than for the Master of a vessel bound for Neath from any part of the world to make the Mumbles Lighthouse, and, with that guide, to get into or off Swansea Bay, where he would meet with Neath Pilots and tugboats, who would take his vessel to Britonferry or Neath, with equal safety, as soon, if not sooner, than to Swansea.[62]

The straightening of the channel was achieved by using hundreds of thousands of tons of copper slag to construct embankments. A great deal of copper slag was used elsewhere upstream towards the town to improve the river banks. The local copper works produced an inexhaustible supply.

In 1861, when a Select Committee of the House of Commons was considering draft legislation to permit the Vale of Neath Railway at Neath to be extended to Swansea by the construction of the Neath to Swansea Direct Railway Line, there was much discussion about a proposed branch of this railway connecting Red Jacket on the Swansea side to Briton Ferry by means of a bridge across the River Neath which would allow coal from the Glyncorrwg district, on the east side of the river, to have direct access to Swansea. There was great concern about the effect this bridge would have on river traffic. Evidence given to the Select Committee provides interesting information.

Captain Lowther, harbourmaster of Neath for the preceding eighteen years, said the 'average tonnage of vessels coming to the port is from 90 to 150 tons,' and about 2,000 vessels enter the port. He described the channel of the river as 'very crooked and very dangerous with a shifting sand bottom; there are frequent floods, and the sand, therefore, is constantly shifting'. He commented that 'a good many of the vessels sail up the river without steam, but if a bridge was placed across the river canvass would be little or no good. It would be a great tax to employ steam in addition to the delay which would be caused.' Richard Prust, shipbroker of Swansea, who had 'been a shipmaster nearly thirty years,' and who knew the Neath River very well, said that the 'trade of Neath is carried on by means of steam-tugs towing vessels; steam-tugs take up six or eight vessels at a time'. He also commented that 'the current runs very strong in Neath, and the sand is shifting'. Two of the Neath Pilots also gave evidence. Jeremiah Gilbert, a pilot at Neath for ten years, said 'a great many [vessels] sail up and a great many are towed up – several together'. Thomas Emmanuel, a pilot at Neath for twenty-four, years, said 'I have frequently taken up five or six vessels with a steam-tug'.

Captain Lowther also said 'one trader of Neath pays nearly one-third of the whole dues – I mean Mr. James Kenway, importer of grain. Mr. Evan Evans also pays large tolls'. He commented further that 'we do not pretend to do much trade at Neath town, only at spring tides, except Mr Evans, who has a steamer running twice a week'.

The proposed branch railway was struck out of the Bill.[63]

Close to the point where the River Neath is joined by the River Clydach there is a significant bend, approximately a right angle. In the 1870s there was a scheme to build a New Cut which would replace this bend in the river with a straight channel up to Neath Bridge and permit the conversion of the original channel thus bypassed into a Floating Dock. Construction work did not commence in earnest until the summer of 1882. A portion of the main channel of the river was blocked from 1 January 1883 and a temporary channel opened to allow ships to pass the New Cut works. A one-way system controlled by red lights and semaphore signals was put in place to allow ships to move up and down river.[64] The New Cut scheme was not successful. In 1884 a severe storm washed away much of the works that had been completed and in due course, after much expenditure, the scheme lapsed. The temporary channel remained in operation until 1 March 1909 when the lights and signalling were discontinued.[65] This scheme must have had some delaying effect on the passage of ships on the river.

CHAPTER 5

The *Neath Abbey*'s Working Life

The Neath to Bristol Service

After completion of fitting out the trip by the shareholders and their friends took place on Monday 27 July when 'a party of holiday-seekers proceeded from the village of Neath Abbey in a newly launched (screw) steam-packet to Tenby, and enjoyed themselves during the day in various ways'.[66]

Advertisements in the *Bristol Mercury* on 1 August and other newspapers marked the commencement of the ship's regular schedule of twice-weekly sailings between Neath and Bristol on 1 August 1846. On that day the ship started 48 years of service on the Bristol Channel.

The new Neath to Bristol service was one of many such cross-channel services. On 1 August 1846 the *Bristol Mercury* also carried advertisements for steamer services from Bristol to Chepstow, Newport, Cardiff, Liverpool (calling at Swansea and Milford), to Dublin (calling at Swansea, Tenby, Milford and other South Wales ports on various days), and between Ilfracombe and Swansea. On 31 July *The Welshman* also advertised sailings between Bristol and Carmarthen (on to Tenby on Tuesdays), Gloucester and Swansea (on to Tenby on Saturdays, returning Sundays), and Gloucester and Newport. At least twelve ships are named in these advertisements. Only three of them were screw steamers: the *Clara*, built at Liverpool in 1842 by John Grantham, the *Henry Southan* and the *Neath Abbey*. The multiplicity of cross-channel services demonstrates the importance of Bristol and, to a lesser extent, Gloucester to the South Wales economy. At both places there were already railway stations.

From the start of the Neath to Bristol service it was advertised that passengers would 'be taken aboard at Briton Ferry, if near the Rock House, fifteen minutes after the advertised time of leaving Neath,' where she berthed at the Town Quay adjacent to the river bridge. The Rock House stood on the left bank of the river, the tide coming up to its sloping lawn and garden. In 1846 when the Briton Ferry Iron Works was built it became the offices of that company.[67]

From July 1848 passengers from Bristol could be landed at the Mumbles if wished.[68] In September 1848 it was advertised that passengers from Neath could be landed at Clevedon if required.[69]

When the service started in August 1846 sailings from Neath were usually on Mondays and Thursdays and on Wednesdays and Saturdays from Bristol. There were variations from time to time and later in the period Tuesdays and Fridays became the more usual days of scheduled sailings from Bristol. Most often the passage across the Channel was direct but there was flexibility depending on cargo shippers' requirements and crossings were made via Swansea, Port Talbot or Cardiff or the voyage was extended to or from Llanelli. Between scheduled sailings there were often local cargo trips from Neath to Swansea, Port Talbot or Llanelli. Some calls at Cardiff or Avonmouth were with cargo to be transferred to a foreign-bound vessel. For example, on 14 July 1882, the *Neath Abbey* arrived at Roath Basin, Cardiff, with tinplates to be loaded on to s.s. *Helmstadt*.[70]

The ship's timetable was governed by the tides. Departure times from Neath in August 1846 varied between five in the morning on 6 August and three in the afternoon on 17 August. The ship left Bathurst Basin, Bristol, at times varying between one o'clock in the morning on 15 August and eleven in the morning on 29 August.

There were occasions when it was necessary to interrupt the ship's routine in order to carry out more substantial repair work than could be managed while she was in port between scheduled sailings. Thus on 21 February 1848 the Agents issued a Notice that the Proprietors of the *Neath Abbey* intended to 'Lay Her Up, on and after 1st of March, 1848, for a Week or Nine Days, to undergo some necessary repairs and painting'.[71] On these occasions it was the usual practice to arrange for a replacement vessel but I have not found any information of such an arrangement on this occasion.

The advertisement for sailings by the *Neath Abbey* in December 1848 included the following statement:

> The *Liverpool Packet* and another Vessel will sail in connexion with the *Neath Abbey* Steam-Packet, and will leave Bristol *once a week*. Parties will do well in ordering by the *Neath Abbey* Steam-Packet Co.'s Sailing

Vessels, as the freights will be moderate. Goods delivered *free of harbour-dues, landing and haulage*, within the delivery of the town, haulage of iron excepted. To ensure the safe delivery of empties a list to be given to the Mate, who will procure a receipt at Bristol.'[72]

Advertisements continued to mention the *Liverpool Packet* and 'another vessel' until June 1849. There is no mention of them again until the beginning of 1852 when William Morgan & Co., Nos. 11 and 12 Welch Back, took over from William Trickey as the Agent at Bristol and placed an advertisement in the *Bristol Times* informing 'Carriers and Shippers of Goods for Neath, Aberdare, Hirwain, Maesteg, Aberavon, Cwmavon, and places adjacent,' that they were now the Agents 'of the Neath Steam Packet Company's Steamer *Neath Abbey*, Schooner *Liverpool Packet* and Smack *Happy Return*. From and after January 1st, 1852, all Goods intended to be sent by the above Vessels will be received daily at the Neath Tier, opposite Mr. Grace's Mill, Welshback'.[73]

The advertisement for January 1852 sailings reflected this, stating that the 'Neath Steam-Packet Company's fine new iron-built Steamer *Neath Abbey* John Williams Commander, in connexion [*sic*] with the Schooner *Liverpool Packet*, John Weslake [*sic*], Master, and Smack *Happy Return*, Thomas Jones, Master, will take in Goods daily at the Welsh-Back, Bristol'.[74]

The *Liverpool Packet* was a 67-ton schooner built at Bideford in 1835 and the *Happy Return* was a 35-ton sloop or smack built at Fowey in 1846.[75]

The January 1852 advertisements suggest that all three of these vessels were owned by the Neath Steam Packet Company. This was not the case. They were owned separately. The first owners of the *Neath Abbey* were three copartners, Evan Evans, Paul Evans French and Jonathan Rees. French died in 1847 and it is probable that his shares passed to Evans who was sole owner not later than 1860. So in 1852 she may have been owned by Evans and Rees. Evan Evans bought 48 shares in the *Liverpool Packet* in 1847. The other 16 were owned by another Neath brewer, John Giles, but they were sold to Evans in October 1849. In 1851 the *Happy Return* was owned jointly by two other Neath businessmen, Thomas Winwood, Flour Merchant, and Edward Boone, Ironmonger.[76]

The last advertisement naming the three ships appears to have been published in June 1852. In July 1852 Thomas and Son were once again the Agents at Bristol in place of William Morgan and Co.[77]

The correct name of the master of the *Liverpool Packet* was John Westlake and he had been master of that ship for a number of years before she was bought by Evans and Giles. He became master of the *Neath Abbey* in August 1852.

Even when the three ships were not linked in advertisements there were a number of reports of the three sailing on the same day from Neath for Bristol or from Bristol for Neath.

On 15 January 1850 the *Liverpool Packet* was on her regular voyage from Neath to Bristol with a cargo of goods, 'consisting of junk, wool, and empty packages,' when she was run down by the paddle steamer *Rose* near Walton Bay, Somerset, and cut 'nearly down to the water's edge. […] The bow-sprit, jib, and jibstay were carried away'. She was towed to Bristol, where she was put into dock, and remained eight weeks undergoing repairs. Evan Evans brought an action against the Bristol Steam Navigation Company, owners of the *Rose*, to recover the cost of repairing the damage done and compensation for the loss which had been sustained during the time she was unable to sail, and was awarded £243 7s.[78]

The *Liverpool Packet*, still owned by Evan Evans, was sailing from Barrow to Cardiff when she foundered off Holyhead after being in collision with the *Bijou* bound for Liverpool on 1 May 1853. The crew were saved.[79]

Between 16 May and 13 October 1865 there are no reports in the *Shipping & Mercantile Gazette* of sailings by the *Neath Abbey* although she is named in frequent advertisments listing her sailings throughout the period.[80] During that time the service must have been operated by another ship. The explanation for the *Neath Abbey*'s absence from reports of sailings is given in the following report.

> The "NEATH ABBEY" STEAMER. – This vessel, belonging to Evan Evans, Esq., of the Vale of Neath Brewery, trading between Neath and Bristol, and which has for some time past been undergoing thorough repair and enlargement, has been completed. In fact she has been so thoroughly overhauled that she may now be deemed a new steamer. Being ready and fully equipped for sea she started on her first voyage since her enlargement on Wednesday morning [11 October], with a full crew and several passengers. She left Neath at about 9 a.m., amid the cheers of a number of spectators, and on her arrival at Britonferry [*sic*] she was greeted by a great crowd of persons assembled on the banks of the river. The *Neath Abbey* never looked so gay before with her new rigging, streamers, and flags flying, as when she stopped her course for taking on board the worthy and respected proprietor; and as Mr Evans passed through the streets of Britonferry he was joined by a number of

the tradesmen, who accompanied him to the boat. When he got on board the steamer, and the vessel began to move, it was the signal for one general shout, and three times three lusty cheers proposed by Mr. Amesbury, of the Villier's [sic] Arms Hotel, were given in the most vociferous and enthusiastic manner. Several friends afterwards adjourned to the Villier's Arms, where they drank health and long life to Captain Evans, and success to their old friend the *Neath Abbey*, although she appeared again with a new face.[81]

Information about the work done is given in Chapter 3. 'Captain Evans' was the owner, Evan Evans. As described in Chapter 8 he was commissioned Captain in the 17th Glamorgan Rifle Volunteers which he set up in 1860. John Westlake was master in 1865.

The List D 'Account of the Voyages and the Crew' for January to June 1872 has a note that the steamer was 'on slip 17 days from May 3/72 to May 20/72 and proceeded to sea on June 3 1872'.[82] There is no information about the reason for this.

Again in 1874 the List D for July to the end of December 1874 noted her 'Laying up from July 1/74 to August 19 1874 at Bristol'. The crew list for the period records that five of the crew had been discharged on 10 June 1874 at Bristol and had been re-engaged on 10 August 1974 at the same port. They were the master, Daniel Evans, the mate, Griffith Evans, two able seamen and the cook. The five other crew men named had sailed on other ships during the previous six months and all were engaged at Bristol on 10 August.[83] This information indicates that the period during which the *Neath Abbey* was laid up began on 10 June, not 1 July. Unfortunately the crew list for January to June 1874 has not survived.

List D for July to December 1883 states that from 28 June to 27 November 1883 the steamer was laid up for the fitting of a new boiler, and that from 28 November to 31 December she was once again sailing between Neath & Bristol with general cargo. She had arrived at Bristol from Neath on June 28, so must have been laid up there.[84] The crew list shows that the master, Henry Davies, and the mate, Thomas Davies, had signed on once again at the beginning of the period, while the other five members of the crew, the engineer, two seamen and two firemen, did not sign on until 28 November.[85] Strangely, there are newspaper reports of her sailing from Bristol to Neath on 2 and 10 August and from Swansea to Bristol on 10 November.[86] So, if these reports are correct, who manned the vessel on those occasions?

In addition to maintaining scheduled twice-weekly sailings between Neath and Bristol the *Neath Abbey* frequently sailed on excursions and a number of these are described in Chapter 7. Furthermore, during the period 1875 to 1877 she not only maintained a limited service between Neath and Bristol but also sailed regularly between Bristol and Bideford or Barnstaple as well as making excursion trips on the Devon and Somerset coasts.

When her period of working on the Somerset and Devon Coast ended, the previous Neath to Bristol frequency was not restored. During the first half of 1878 the Half-yearly Agreement records the ship sailing three times a fortnight between Bristol and Neath and once a fortnight between Bristol and Barnstaple.[87] During both halves of 1884 notes on List D describe the *Neath Abbey* as trading between Neath and Bristol three times a fortnight.[88]

Because of winding up proceedings brought against the then owners, the Neath and Bristol Steamship Company, sailings between Neath and Bristol stopped in November 1887 and the *Neath Abbey* did not sail again until August 1890 when she started a service between Swansea and Bristol. From time to time during this period the ship called at Briton Ferry. This service is described below. It was maintained until the ship was wrecked in June 1894.

Advertisements for the Neath to Bristol service that appeared until the end of 1865, after which I have not found similar advertisements, continued to state that the *Neath Abbey* would call at Briton Ferry to pick up passengers fifteen minutes after leaving Neath. From 1 April 1861 it was advertised that 'Goods for Briton Ferry will be discharged into a Warehouse solely for that purpose near the Ferry'.[89] The map of Briton Ferry illustrated shows the position of the Steam Packet Wharf on the riverside slightly upstream of the Ferry (see Illustration 10, page 104). The acquisition of this warehouse was in anticipation of completion of the Briton Ferry Dock which was opened on 22 August 1861, 'a wet and unfavourable day'.

> The town of Britton [*sic*] Ferry put on a very gay appearance, triumphal arches, flags, banners, &c., were met in every direction. The *Neath Abbey* steamer, gaily decorated with flags, was the first vessel to enter the dock. A special train arrived and deposited a number of passengers, while on the opposite side of the harbour an engine conducted a train of coal to the float for shipment, and to receive which there were three vessels (one a Yankee, the *Mary Stetson*), the *Alnwick*, and the *Reaper*, on the opposite side. The Briton Ferry Artillery fired a royal salute. The Neath Rifles on one side, and Brewery Rifles the other, also fired. The bands

played the National Anthem, and several cheers proclaimed the opening of the Briton Ferry Dock for shipping.[90]

Neath Abbey on the Somerset and Devon Coast

In his description of the Bristol to Bideford and Barnstaple Passenger Services Grahame Farr wrote that there 'was a short-lived project during May-July 1876, with the *Neath Abbey*, owned by Rees, Evans and French of Neath, which usually ran between Neath and Bristol'.[91]

This statement is incorrect. The *Neath Abbey* operated on this West Country route from June 1875 to the end of 1877 and to a lesser extent during the first seven months of 1878. No record has been found of her sailing on that route after 31 July. Furthermore, Rees, Evans and French were the joint owners of the ship when she was launched in 1846 but by 1865 Evan Evans was the sole owner and on his death in 1871 his daughter Mary Bevan inherited the ship.

In May 1875, it was reported that 'the owners of the screw steamer *Neath Abbey* intend to run her between Bristol, Ilfracombe and Bideford, with goods and passengers. The first trip will be made on Tuesday, and it is intended that the service shall be continuous. She will be commanded by Captain Clibbett. The undertaking will supply a want long felt, and will materially improve the means of communication between the two latter towns'. In the same edition of the newspaper the *Neath Abbey* was advertised to sail from Bristol to Ilfracombe and Bideford on Tuesday 1 June and every following Tuesday and to return from Bideford to Ilfracombe, Lynmouth and Bristol on Wednesday 2 June and every following Wednesday.[92]

Although the fact does not appear to have been mentioned in newspapers it is worth noting that James Clibbett who became master of the *Neath Abbey* in May 1875 was from Appledore, quite close to both Bideford and Barnstaple. Was he influential in arranging this West Country service?

The local paper reported the arrival of the *Neath Abbey* on its first trip to Bideford on 1 June 1875.

> Our port on Tuesday had a more business-like appearance than we have seen for some time. The *Neath Abbey*, which had been put on the station, arrived on her first trip about four p.m., and as she was commenced to be discharged immediately on her arrival, the smack,

Ann, which has also only recently been put on the station, discharging her goods at the same time, the Quay was soon lined with a lot of merchandise.[93]

The same issue of the newspaper also reported the death of Captain Daniel Walters, the owner and master of the *Ann*, who was found drowned in the Basin at Bristol on 26 May and commented:

> It was a melancholy coincidence that the deceased's vessel, the *Ann*, which he had only so recently commanded on her trip to Bristol for goods, should have been laying alongside of the quay here on Tuesday discharging, when the remains of deceased were brought home on board the steamer *Neath Abbey*, on her first trip to Bideford, and which deceased thought was put on the station in opposition to himself.

Daniel Walters was a coal merchant of Westleigh, two miles from Bideford, and had been missing for several days after going ashore from the *Ann* at Bristol and visiting 'the "Sedan Chair" a very celebrated resort for Devonshire captains'. It was thought that while going back to his vessel he fell into the water and was drowned.[94]

In 1875 *Neath Abbey* fares between Lynmouth, Ilfracombe, or Bideford and Bristol were Best Cabin 6s., Second Cabin 4s. A return ticket available for a fortnight cost 9s. or 6s. Between Lynmouth, Ilfracombe and Bideford passengers could either buy a ticket for the Cabin for 2s. or travel on deck for 1s. As usual, children under 12 years of age were charged half price. To or from Bideford and Bristol other rates were horses 20s., sheep and lambs 1s., pigs 1s. 6d., dogs 2s., carriages 42s., phaetons 25s. and gigs 1s.[95]

Two changes were made to this service. In October 1875 a once-weekly call at Ilfracombe was introduced.[96] J. W. Pockett's Steamers of Swansea were already operating a frequent service between Padstow, Swansea and Ilfracombe.[97] The second change was in March 1877 when it was reported that 'The *Neath Abbey*, hitherto trading between Bristol and Bideford with goods and passengers, has commenced to make Barnstaple her port of destination, instead of Bideford, owing to insufficient traffic there and bad laying ground'. The ship sailed from Bristol on Fridays and returned on Saturdays.[98]

The first voyage to Barnstaple was on 16 March 1877.

> THE SCREW STEAMER *Neath Abbey* arrived at our Quay on Friday evening last at 8 pm from Bristol, with a cargo of general goods

for the different tradesmen of the town, which was landed the same night, the steamer leaving again with Saturday morning's tide. The goods were all delivered on Saturday. Although blowing strongly from the westward the staunch little craft, through the perseverance of her experienced and able commander, Captain James Clibbett, sped her way down Channel and in over the Bar to Appledore pool, where she was boarded by our old and experienced river pilot, Mr Joseph Stribling, sen., and was safely brought, amidst the roar of cannon, alongside our quay. It has been the wish of the tradesmen of Barnstaple, for many years past, to get a steamer to come direct from Bristol to our quay with their goods, instead of barging them from Bideford. They now have their wish complied with, and there is one thing wanted to retain her on the station, which is to give her that support which will be remunerative to her owner and agent, whose study will be, we are assured, to give every care and speedy delivery to goods placed in their charge. The *Neath Abbey* will load at Bristol once a fortnight on the spring tides for Barnstaple Quay.[99]

Throughout the period while the *Neath Abbey* was sailing regularly between Bristol and West Country ports, she also maintained a service between Bristol and Neath, although the frequency was reduced and varied from month to month. The shipping intelligence information published of sailings and arrivals at Neath and Bristol is not exhaustive. During the months of 1875, after the service began, published reports show the number of trips varying between nine in July and three in September. In 1876 the number identified varied between four and seven, with the exception of December, in which only two have been identified. *The Neath Tide Table for 1876* had an advertisement that the *Neath Abbey* Steam Packet sailed regularly once a week between Bristol and Neath, loading at Welsh Back, Bristol, every Monday. 'Fares: Best Cabin, 4s.; Second Cabin 2s. 6d. Rates for Goods on Application'.[100]

In December 1876 and January 1877 advertisements for the service between Bristol, Ilfracombe and Bideford listed four sailings a month between those places, three sailings a month from Neath to Bristol and one sailing a month from Ilfracombe to Neath.[101] The poster advertising 'Steam Communication between Bristol, Neath, Ilfracombe, and Bideford' enables the *Neath Abbey*'s schedule of sailings for January 1877 to be listed chronologically.[102] See Illustration 6 overleaf.

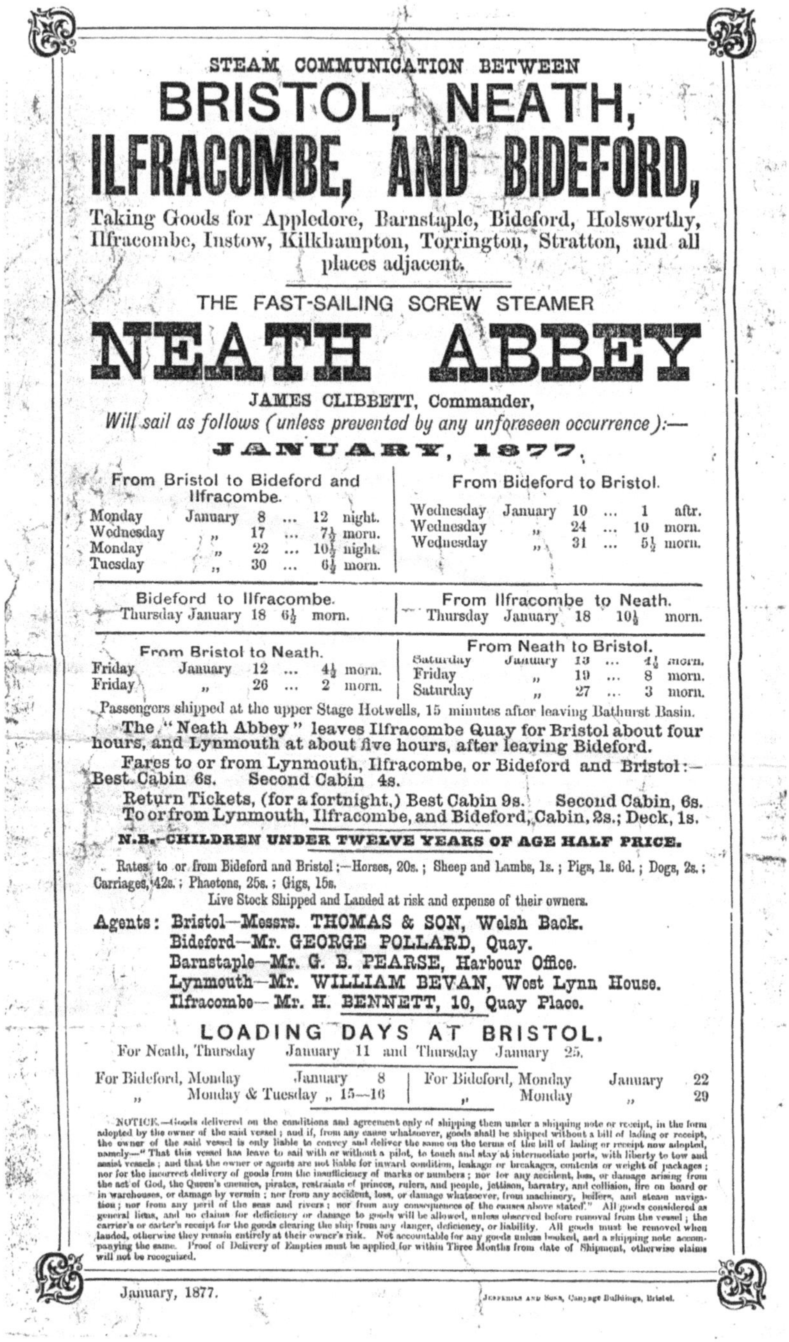

STEAM COMMUNICATION BETWEEN

BRISTOL, NEATH, ILFRACOMBE, AND BIDEFORD,

Taking Goods for Appledore, Barnstaple, Bideford, Holsworthy, Ilfracombe, Instow, Kilkhampton, Torrington, Stratton, and all places adjacent.

THE FAST-SAILING SCREW STEAMER

NEATH ABBEY

JAMES CLIBBETT, Commander,

Will sail as follows (unless prevented by any unforeseen occurrence):—

JANUARY, 1877.

From Bristol to Bideford and Ilfracombe.

Monday	January	8	...	12 night.
Wednesday	„	17	...	7½ morn.
Monday	„	22	...	10½ night.
Tuesday	„	30	...	6½ morn.

From Bideford to Bristol.

Wednesday	January	10	...	1 aftr.
Wednesday	„	24	...	10 morn.
Wednesday	„	31	...	5½ morn.

Bideford to Ilfracombe.
Thursday January 18 6½ morn.

From Ilfracombe to Neath.
Thursday January 18 10½ morn.

From Bristol to Neath.

Friday	January	12	...	4½ morn.
Friday	„	26	...	2 morn.

From Neath to Bristol.

Saturday	January	13	...	4½ morn.
Friday	„	19	...	8 morn.
Saturday	„	27	...	3 morn.

Passengers shipped at the upper Stage Hotwells, 15 minutes after leaving Bathurst Basin.

The "Neath Abbey" leaves Ilfracombe Quay for Bristol about four hours, and Lynmouth at about five hours, after leaving Bideford.

Fares to or from Lynmouth, Ilfracombe, or Bideford and Bristol:— Best Cabin 6s. Second Cabin 4s.

Return Tickets, (for a fortnight,) Best Cabin 9s. Second Cabin, 6s. To or from Lynmouth, Ilfracombe, and Bideford, Cabin, 2s.; Deck, 1s.

N.B.—CHILDREN UNDER TWELVE YEARS OF AGE HALF PRICE.

Rates to or from Bideford and Bristol:—Horses, 20s.; Sheep and Lambs, 1s.; Pigs, 1s. 6d.; Dogs, 2s.; Carriages, 42s.; Phaetons, 25s.; Gigs, 15s.

Live Stock Shipped and Landed at risk and expense of their owners.

Agents: Bristol—Messrs. THOMAS & SON, Welsh Back.
Bideford—Mr. GEORGE POLLARD, Quay.
Barnstaple—Mr. G. B. PEARSE, Harbour Office.
Lynmouth—Mr. WILLIAM BEVAN, West Lynn House.
Ilfracombe—Mr. H. BENNETT, 10, Quay Place.

LOADING DAYS AT BRISTOL.

For Neath, Thursday January 11 and Thursday January 25.

For Bideford, Monday January 8
„ Monday & Tuesday „ 15—16

For Bideford, Monday January 22
„ Monday „ 29

NOTICE.—Goods delivered on the conditions and agreement only of shipping them under a shipping note or receipt, in the form adopted by the owner of the said vessel; and if, from any cause whatsoever, goods shall be shipped without a bill of lading or receipt, the owner of the said vessel is only liable to convey and deliver the same on the terms of the bill of lading or receipt now adopted, namely—"That this vessel has leave to sail with or without a pilot, to touch and stay at intermediate ports, with liberty to tow and assist vessels; and that the owner or agents are not liable for inward condition, leakage or breakages, contents or weight of packages; nor for the incorrect delivery of goods from the insufficiency of marks or numbers; nor for any accident, loss, or damage arising from the act of God, the Queen's enemies, pirates, restraints of princes, rulers, and people, jettison, barratry, and collision, fire on board or in warehouses, or damage by vermin; nor from any accident, loss, or damage whatsoever, from machinery, boilers, and steam navigation; nor from any peril of the seas and rivers; nor from any consequences of the causes above stated." All goods considered as general liens, and no claims for deficiency or damage to goods will be allowed, unless observed before removal from the vessel; the carrier's or carter's receipt for the goods clearing the ship from any danger, deficiency, or liability. All goods must be removed when landed, otherwise they remain entirely at their owner's risk. Not accountable for any goods unless booked, and a shipping note accompanying the same. Proof of Delivery of Empties must be applied for within Three Months from date of Shipment, otherwise claims will not be recognized.

January, 1877.

Jefferies and Sons, Cambridge Buildings, Bristol.

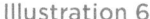

Illustration 6
Poster for Bristol, Neath, Ilfracombe and Bideford service, 1877.

January

8	12.00 midnight	Bristol to Bideford and Ilfracombe.
10	1.00 p.m.	Bideford to Bristol
12	4.30 a.m.	Bristol to Neath
13	4.30 a.m.	Neath to Bristol
17	7.30 a.m.	Bristol to Bideford and Ilfracombe
18	6.30 a.m.	Bideford to Ilfracombe
	10.30 a.m.	Ilfracombe to Neath
19	8.00 a.m.	Neath to Bristol
22	10.30 p.m.	Bristol to Bideford and Ilfracombe
24	10.00 a.m.	Bideford to Bristol
26	2.00 a.m.	Bristol to Neath
27	3.00 a.m.	Neath to Bristol
30	6.30 a.m.	Bristol to Bideford and Ilfracombe.
31	5.30 a.m.	Bideford to Bristol

During 1877 shipping intelligence reports show that the monthly number varied between three and seven apart from one in February and one in March but, as already mentioned, such reports are not exhaustive.

The half-yearly Crew Agreement for the first half of 1878 has a note by the master, James Clibbett, that during the period the ship was trading three times a fortnight between Bristol and Neath and once a fortnight between Bristol and Barnstaple.[103] The Crew List for the second half of 1878 has the statement 'Trading between Bristol and [sic] three times a fortnight'. Shipping intelligence reports for the second half of 1878 mention *Neath Abbey* sailing to or from Barnstaple three times and Appledore twice in July but not at all afterwards. Thus the port name missing from the Crew List is Neath. (The Agreements and Crew Lists for 1875 to 1877 are not available.)

In February 1878, Mr Cornelius Griffith, formerly the proprietor of the *Ilfracombe Chronicle*, brought an action in the County Court at Barnstaple against George Pollard, agent for the *Neath Abbey* at Bideford, to recover the sum of £2 14s. in respect of advertisements relative to the ship. The advertisements had appeared from October 1875 until nearly the end of the following year. Mr Pollard claimed that he had only intended the advertisement to appear for one month, but Mr Griffith claimed that subsequently he had received postcards from Pollard requesting alterations and one of these dating from January 1876, four months after the advertisement had first appeared, was produced in evidence. Judgment was given for the plaintiff.[104]

While the ship was operating this service she sailed on many West Country excursions. These are described in Chapter 7.

Carmarthen to Bristol

An advertisement in December 1880 for Steam Communication between Bristol and Carmarthen included the following information:

> The Llanelly Steam Navigation Company, Limited, beg to announce that at the request of influential Firms interested in the Trade between the above Ports, the Fast New Iron Screw Steamer, The "NEATH ABBEY" (Being fitted with a new boiler, and the machinery put in thoroughly efficient order WILLIAM THOMAS, Commander, is intended to Sail as follows (with goods only). Loading Days at Bristol. On Saturday, 18th December, 1880. Sheep conveyed at 1s., Pigs 1s. All Goods to be alongside the Packet before five o' clock p.m.[105]

This is a strange and misleading advertisement. The *Neath Abbey* was not being fitted with a new boiler or having her machinery put in order. She was kept busy throughout 1880 sailing between Neath and Bristol as usual.

The Llanelly Steam Navigation Company was formed in January 1863 with the small steamer *Leopard* and had the larger *Cambria* built at Llanelli in 1866 by Nevill and Company. Both ships were Bristol Channel coasters sailing mainly on the Llanelli, Swansea, Bristol route.[106] The *Cambria* had a new boiler fitted in September 1872 and was temporarily replaced by the *Express* until she returned to service on 1 October.[107] The first advertisement found for the Bristol to Carmarthen service was on 4 April 1873.[108]

From May 1873 until at least October 1883 all advertisements for the Bristol to Llanelli or Carmarthen service were unchanged apart from the dates of the Loading Days and when the *Cambria* was temporarily replaced by another vessel, the name of that ship. Advertisements on 27 September and 4 October 1878 name the *St. Vincent* as the replacement. On 17 December 1880, 21 January 1881, 24 March, 5 May, and 15 September 1882, and 26 January 1883, the *Neath Abbey* was named in place of the *Cambria*. In every advertisement until at least November 1883, whether for sailings by the *Cambria*, the *St. Vincent* or the *Neath Abbey*, the ship was described as a 'Fast New Iron Screw Steamer' and as being 'fitted with a new boiler, and the machinery put in thoroughly efficient order'. Almost all the advertisements gave Loading Days earlier than the date of publication. In all advertisements it is stated that she was intended to sail with goods only. It is clear that references after October 1872 to the *Cambria* or a replacement vessel being fitted with a new boiler are wrong.

The owner of the *Neath Abbey* during the years mentioned was Mary Bevan and it must be assumed that, acting through her husband David Bevan, she allowed the ship to be hired to replace the *Cambria* on the dates advertised. In the case of such hiring it would be expected that the ship would have been commanded by her regular master, either Clibbett or Davies, during those years, and not by William Thomas, the master of the *Cambria*.

During all this time the *Neath Abbey* was sailing between Neath and Bristol. J. L. Matthews was the agent for her throughout. A search of newspaper records of sailings by the *Neath Abbey* during 1880, 1881, 1882 and 1883 has found only two mentions of Carmarthen. On 16 June 1882, she was cleared from Neath and Briton Ferry for Carmarthen with general cargo and she was reported to have arrived at Bristol from Carmarthen on 14 January 1883.[109] Neither date corresponds with an advertised loading date for the *Neath Abbey*. However, it may be that sailings between Carmarthen and Bristol via Llanelli were recorded in the newspapers as between Bristol and Llanelli. There are several such records. For example, in 1881 sailings are recorded on 27 February,[110] 25 April, 10 May, 15 May, 10 June, 1 & 22 November and 9 December.[111]

1886–1890

The *Neath Abbey* continued to sail regularly between Neath and Bristol until November 1887. Occasionally longer trips are mentioned such as Burry Port or Llanelli to Gloucester, Llanelli to Liverpool, and between South Wales ports. In 1886 the Neath and Bristol Steamship Company purchased the vessel from Mary Bevan. This transfer of ownership is dealt with in Chapter 13.

There is no record of sailings between 18 November 1887, when she sailed from Bristol for Llanelli and 10 March 1890, when the *Bristol Mercury* reported that she had arrived at Bristol from Llanelli on 9 March.[112] This was because the Neath and Bristol Steamship Company was in financial difficulty.

The Account of Voyages for the period 1 January to 30 June 1890, signed by the master, Henry Davies, has the following manuscript notes:

> The "Neath Abbey" was laid up at Llanelly, from November 17, 1887, until March 19, 1890 […] when she arrived at Bristol, for repairs,

which occupied from that date, until August 7 1890, when she loaded a general cargo at Bristol for Swansea.

No crew on board.[113]

(The date of March 19, 1890, may be an error by Davies. The *Bristol Mercury* reported that she arrived at Bristol on Sunday, 9 March.[114])

The reason for laying the ship up was that in 1887 D. A. W. Baile, a creditor of the company, brought a petition in the Liverpool District Registry for winding up the company on the ground of its insolvency. In evidence at the hearing in December it was stated that in April the company had admitted liability to Mr. Baile in the sum of £1,265 9s. 2d. and that since then further sums of money had been advanced by him. Application had been made for payment of the debt but without effect. The ship was mortgaged to cover a sum of £700. In addition there were three other creditors with claims totalling £450 as well as others. Evidence was given that 'the registered offices of the company at Neath had been closed for some time, and the service of the petition had been effected by pushing it under the door and by taking a duplicate copy of it to Messrs Thomas and Son at Welsh Back, Bristol, who had been for a long time conducting the business of the company'.[115]

In late January 1888 Mr. Justice Kekewich made an order for the winding up of the company.[116]

Nothing more was reported of the ship until 1890 when Messrs. Short and Dunn of Cardiff advertised that on 28 April they would auction the *Neath Abbey*, 'now lying at Bristol where she may be seen,' at the Dowlais Hotel, Bute Docks, Cardiff.[117] 'There was a fair attendance of local merchants and others at the auction and the price realised was £325'.[118] In 1891, via a series of transactions described in Chapter 13, the *Neath Abbey* was purchased by Robert Harding Gunning.[119]

Swansea to Bristol

In August 1890 it was reported that the *Neath Abbey*, 'a commodious and well-fitted boat,' would in future run regularly between Swansea and Bristol. There would be seven journeys each way in August. The ship was described as 'fitted to carry all kinds of goods, as well as livestock' at most moderate charges. Information was available from Mr. H. Gunning, Broad Quay, Swansea.[120] It seems that the service was intended to be for goods only.

The *Neath Abbey* arrived at the North Dock, Swansea on 8 August from Bristol with sundries.[121] Throughout the rest of the year there are reports of her sailing between Bristol and Swansea with at least some calls at Port Talbot.

Advertisements in August show that sailings in each direction were in the afternoon or evening.[122] During the months of September 1890 to March 1891, after which I have found no advertisement, advertisements show that eight or nine sailings were scheduled each month, nearly all in the afternoon or evening. Crew Lists for the next three years state that she was sailing between Bristol and Swansea 'regularly' or 'weekly' but only three of them describe her as sailing twice a week.[123]

For the rest of her life the *Neath Abbey* continued to sail between Swansea and Bristol. Occasionally voyages were extended to or from Gloucester via Bristol and sometimes to or from Llanelli via Swansea. Sometimes she sailed between Swansea and South Wales ports such as Newport and Neath/Briton Ferry. In newspaper reports of departures and arrivals cargoes were most frequently described as general but there are references to cargoes of coal or bunkers (coal for use as ships' fuel), wheat, barley, maize, coal, copper, copper ore, calamine, spelter and tinplates.

An extract from the Official Log of the *Neath Abbey* records an 'Occurrence' off Portishead on 14 July 1893 when the ship was sailing from Bristol to Swansea with general cargo. A machinery breakdown occurred at eight in the evening and on the following day she was towed into Portishead for the machinery to be repaired.[124]

Unusually the ship sailed from Swansea to Roscoff in July 1893 and picked up a cargo of potatoes.[125] In the Log Book for the period 30 June 1893 to 3 January 1894 which includes a printed note requiring this 'List is to be filled up and signed by the Owner or Master of every Home Trade Vessel under 80 tons', Henry Davies, the master, wrote 'Trading between Swansea and Bristol' and also:

> Made one Voyage Swansea to Roscoff France
> Sailed from Swansea 20th-7-93
> Sailed from Roscoff for Swansea July 24th 93
> Arrived at Swansea July 26th 1893
>   No British Consul at Roscoff
>   Captn. H. Davies

That voyage was not 'in the home trade'. As a result Henry Davies had to write to the Superintendent, Board of Trade, Swansea, saying that he was 'not aware that he was breaking the law […] for voyage to Roscoff. Had I known that I required a Log Book & proper Articles, I would have willingly complied with the Law. I beg to state it was quite an oversight. I have been in the Bristol Trade for over 4 years so thought the same Articles would do'. This letter of Explanation was forwarded from Swansea to the Registrar General of Seamen in London with a note requesting 'authority to issue Clearance'. The Registrar's Office replied to the Superintendent at Swansea requesting him to Caution the master and grant clearance.[126] 'Clearance' was a Clearance Certificate which had to be delivered to the Custom House before leaving port. While masters of ships engaged in the home trade were required to complete a report every six months listing the voyages and crew during the preceding half-year, masters of foreign-going vessels were required to file a report on returning to port from each voyage. So Davies should have filed an appropriate report on returning to Swansea from France on 26 July. Also it is probable that he was only qualified to command a ship sailing in the home trade.

On 26 January 1894 the *Neath Abbey* arrived at Bristol with general goods from Swansea. At the mouth of the River Avon, the piston rod of the port cylinder had snapped, 'breaking cylinder cover and two and four studs'. The ship was towed up to the dock after a delay of about two hours.[127] She was back in service not later than 12 February when she sailed from Bristol to Swansea.[128] Cross-channel cargo voyages continued until mid-June 1894 when the *Neath Abbey* was wrecked. An account of her last days is given in Chapter 16.

CHAPTER 6

Passenger Traffic

When the *Neath Abbey* began sailing between Neath and Bristol on 1 August 1846 fares for passengers were First Cabin 7s. 6d.; Second Cabin 4s.; Children under 12 Half-fare. These cabins were not individual cabins but communal saloons where refreshments could be obtained at reasonable prices. Passengers were not expected to pay a 'fee' or gratuity to the Steward or Stewardess.

The passenger fares between Neath and Bristol may be compared with fares on other cross-channel routes during July and August 1846:

Chepstow and Bristol	After Cabin 4s. Fore Deck 1s. 6d.
Newport and Bristol	After Cabin 2s. Fore Cabin 1s.
Cardiff and Bristol Reduced Fares	After Cabin 4s. Fore Cabin 2s.
Swansea and Bristol Reduced Fares	Best Cabin 10s. Fore Cabin 5s.
Swansea and Ilfracombe	Best Cabin, 10s. Fore Cabin, 5s.

Children under 12 years of age half price on all routes.

'To and Fro' fares were offered on some routes at a small reduction on the cost of two one-way fares, but it was necessary to sail in both directions on the same day.

One wonders who could afford these fares. Employment in the Neath district was mainly in the coal, iron and copper industries. Wages fluctuated violently in the first two of these and most of all 'in the remuneration of colliers employed in the mining of sea-sale coal, a trade in which natural conditions varied dramatically, often completely changing the market situation. Thus in 1831, colliers in the neighbourhood of Swansea were being paid 21s. a week, the following year they were averaging 2s. 10¾d., in 1837 3s. 10¼d., and in 1842 3s. 7½d.'.[129] At the 'Cwm Avon Iron, Coal, Copper, Tin, And Chemical Works, Four Miles From Neath' in 1846 the 'earnings of the colliers and miners, who work regularly six days in the week, are from 20s. to 24s. per week, boys 8s. to 10s. The highest paid class of workmen, some of those engaged about the copper works, earn as much as £16 per month. The average of all in that department is 35s. All contribute 4½d. per week to the doctor and sick fund'.[130] During the same year in evidence before a Parliamentary Committee considering a bill to authorise construction of the Vale of Neath Railway Mr. White, F.C.S. who lived at Dowlais, said that he had 'about a hundred patients under his care daily, at ironworks and collieries. The highest wages were about 30s. a week, and the lowest about 11s. a week'.[131] It was reported in 1846 that at the Neath Abbey Iron Works the deductions from wages to contribute towards the cost of schooling were 'trifling' when compared to the wages, which varied from 15s. to 25s. per week, 'often much higher' and that there was 'fuel gratis in many instances'.[132] In April 1846 at the Carmarthenshire Quarter Sessions it was agreed to increase the salary of second class police constables from 16s. to 18s. a week, the same as in Glamorganshire.[133] In May additional police constables were appointed for the Merthyr District at a salary of 20s. per week and 'an additional Turnkey [was] appointed at the House of Correction at Swansea, at the salary of 12s. per week'.[134] The annual salaries offered for the Master and Matron of the Union Workhouse at Neath in 1846 were £40 for the Master and £20 for the Matron 'with the accustomed rations', 'a Man and Wife without incumbrance' preferred. The Master was required to be 'a good penman, and well-versed in accounts and conversant with the Welsh language'[135]. In November 1847 an unnamed 'Iron Works in the neighbourhood of Neath' advertised for 'a respectable Young Man as Third Clerk. One who has been employed in the office of an Iron Works for at least two years, and can produce testimonials as to character and ability, will have a preference. Salary for the first year, £40. A knowledge of the Welsh language is indispensable'.[136] By comparison the Chief Constable of Glamorgan, Captain Napier, was paid a quarterly salary of £112 10s.[137]

As time passed the fares between Neath and Bristol changed. A fare of 6d. for passengers from Neath to Briton Ferry, 'landing included,' was advertised for the first time in October 1846.[138] In January 1847 a charge of 12s. 6d. for a horse was advertised.[139] Gigs 12s., phætons 15s. and carriages 25s. were added to the list in June 1848.[140] In August 1850 passenger fares were reduced to Best Cabin 5s. and Second Cabin 2s. 6d.[141] The fares were reduced to 4s. and 2s. in April 1853 but in June 1860 the Second Cabin fare was 2s. 6d. again.[142] In September 1871 the fares were Best Cabin 4s., Second Cabin 2s. 6d., horses 10s., gigs 10s., phætons 12s. and carriages 20s.[143] Children under 12 years of age always travelled at half fare.

Reports of passenger traffic are few.

In 1847 the arrival on the *Neath Abbey* of the Earl of Jersey, a substantial landowner in the Briton Ferry area, attracted attention. He came with two of his sons, his heir, the Viscount Villiers, MP, and the Hon. Captain Villiers, together with another local land owner, Mr. S. Stanley. The Earl 'inspected his valuable and improving estate' on Tuesday with his agent, Adam Murray, Esq., and others. He and his sons were reported to be staying with H. J. Grant, Esq., at the Gnoll, Grant's mansion overlooking the town of Neath.[144]

In addition to the facility mentioned in early advertisements for the ship to call at Clevedon or the Mumbles if required and following the completion of a Pier at Portishead in the summer of 1868 it was advertised that the *Neath Abbey* would call there if required, giving passengers the opportunity to shorten the passage by ship and catch a train from Portishead to Bristol for a connection to London.[145]

On 2 September 1871 Mr Septimus Moore and two friends travelled on the *Neath Abbey* in order to go to Bristol. It is not surprising that he was annoyed when, after leaving Neath, he learned that on that occasion the ship was sailing via Ilfracombe. He wrote a letter to the Editor of the *Western Mail* setting out his complaint.[146]

> TO THE EDITOR OF THE "WESTERN MAIL."
>
> SIR, – On behalf of other travellers who may be deceived by advertisements, I take the opportunity of telling my experience to you in relation to the *Neath Abbey* steamer. I found in "Bradshaw" that the *Neath Abbey* sailed from Neath to Bristol in six hours on Wednesday and Saturday. In the local advertisements of the vessel's sailings, the above statement is virtually repeated, but the six hours is given as an average passage, and in relation to carrying goods, the owners protect themselves by claiming liberty to tow and assist vessels in distress, as well as to touch and stay at intermediate ports.
>
> Accompanied by two others, I arrived in Neath on Friday last [1 Sept.], after a short stay at Aberavon (one of the places from which, in the local advertisements, the *Neath Abbey* offers the quickest and cheapest route to Bristol), to take passage by this vessel.
>
> On going on board on Saturday morning, I simply asked whether the vessel were going to Bristol, and was told she was. After starting, I discovered that the agent was on board (a Mr. Mathews [*sic*], I believe), and that for his benefit and that of a friend the vessel was to cross the Bristol Channel to Ilfracombe. On the passage across I represented to

this person, in the presence of the captain, that it was a most unwarrantable proceeding for a vessel to be advertised to sail from Neath to Bristol in six hours, and instead of doing so, to cross first to Ilfracombe. He received the remonstration without a word of apology, simply telling me that it had not occurred, I think he said for ten years, and that I should be at Portishead at five o'clock, in time for the last train to London from Bristol. This gentleman's selfishness, not to say breach of faith with the public, reached a climax when he landed in the ship's boat, though a shore boat offered its service alongside the vessel, thus detaining the steamer another twenty minutes to save his dignity, or his pocket, I know not which.

Later in the voyage the captain informed me quite coolly, as a thing to be expected, that we should not reach Portishead until nearly an hour after the last train for London had left. His statement (for reasons I will not enter on) not only made me very indignant, but very anxious. I represented to him that if we did not catch that train, his owners, under the circumstances, would be liable to pay our hotel bill till Monday morning. This, or a consideration of my anxiety (for he was apparently a kindly man), caused him to hasten the speed of his vessel, and he just got us into the train by keeping it waiting a quarter of an hour with his whistle.

I am bound to say that the vessel is a smart craft, the crew to match; but there is no excuse for the agent, who kept the vessel back at least three hours for his own personal convenience, and contrary to his advertisement. This act extended a voyage of nominally six hours to Bristol into one of ten hours to Portishead, keeping his passengers all this time without a regular meal, and preventing us from catching the 3.50 train, on which I reasonably counted. Allow me to add that there was nothing in the weather to make the passage other than an average one to Portishead.

Trusting to your courtesy to expose the above breach of faith, – I remain, yours. &c,
Sept. 5th, 1871.　　　　　　　　SEPTIMUS P. MOORE, LL.B.

The scheduled departure time from Neath on 2 September 1871 was 7.30 a.m., and the captain, the 'kindly man', was Daniel Evans.

Clearly the Great Western Railway staff at Portishead understood the blowing of the ship's whistle as a request to hold back the train until the *Neath Abbey* arrived and disembarked passengers.

CHAPTER 7

Excursions

Excursionists' Experiences and Local Reaction

The introduction of steam-powered vessels on the cross-channel routes reduced voyage times and made it more practicable to run 'marine' or 'aquatic' excursions.

Although there was an excursion from Bristol to Swansea and Tenby in May 1817[147] and a number in the 1820s it was not until the 1830s that there was real development of excursion traffic. In the 1840s growth of this seasonal opportunity to boost ships' earnings was rapid. Previously leisure travel had been something which could only be afforded by people who were sufficiently wealthy to have not only the money but also the time to spare for it. Many people in South Wales had spent their lives able to see the English coastline across the water without any hope of ever visiting it. Now as the number of excursions and the speed of the ships increased there were opportunities to take a break lasting less than twenty-four hours at a price within the pocket of a great many working people and visit that previously unreachable coast.

It was common practice for a special excursion to be arranged to try out and demonstrate a new ship before she started on her regular work. In 1824 the *Lord Beresford*, a wooden paddle steamer, built at Bristol in 1824 and fitted with two 30hp engines at Neath Abbey Iron Works took 'a numerous and very respectable company of Ladies and Gentlemen for an excursion in Swansea Bay' on 8 June. The engines were reported to 'propel her along at the rate of 10 or 11 miles an hour, without producing any unpleasant sensation'. After an hour or two sailing in the Bay the passengers had 'a very comfortable breakfast, handsomely provided for the occasion'.[148]

Over the years the popularity of excursions increased as more and more cross-channel steamers came into service and their reliability improved. Excursions gave many people who might not have been able to afford the fares for scheduled services, opportunities to experience trips on these

43

steamers. During summer months passenger excursions became an important part of the business of ships from both sides of the Bristol Channel and must have made a significant contribution to the financial results achieved for the owners. Ships based at Cardiff, Neath, Swansea and other ports sailed on excursions to Barnstaple, Bideford, Watchet, Weston-super-Mare and most frequently to Ilfracombe on the English side, as well as to Tenby and sometimes to the Royal Dockyard at Pembroke on the Welsh side. Ships from Bristol ran excursions to Cardiff, Swansea and Tenby as well as along the English coast. A feature of many excursions was the presence of a band travelling with the passengers and playing on board and on shore. However, excursionists had to accept departure and arrival times that could be inconvenient because of dependence on the tides and to be prepared for the possibility of bad weather.

On 18 June 1833 there was an excursion from Swansea on board the *Bristol*, a paddle steamer sailing regularly between Bristol and Swansea, to Pater, as Pembroke Dock was then known, so that people could see the launching of the *Rodney*, 92 guns, 'the longest vessel in the British Navy'. She left Swansea at four o'clock in the morning and returned in the evening. The fares were Cabin 12s. and Steerage 7s. It was reported that there was excellent music on board, 'entertainment provided by the steward, and the obliging offices rendered by the stewardess to the ladies, gave the utmost satisfaction'. 'A little sea-sickness' was attributed to the windy weather but the excursionists were delighted by the 'grand spectacle' at Pater and the splendid scenery.[149]

While many excursions were arranged by the steam packet owners or agents, others were organised by private groups that chartered a ship for the occasion. Some examples follow.

In June 1844 the Committee of the Widow and Orphan's Fund of the Carmarthen and District Oddfellows advertised that they had arranged their annual excursion to Tenby on board the *Phoenix*. The ship left Carmarthen Quay at six in the morning, picked up passengers at the Ferry at Llanstephan and the mouth of the Kidwelly and Laugharne Rivers and the Carmarthen Brass Band travelled with them. Fares were 'Cabin Passengers (without any extra charge) 4s.; Deck Passengers 3s.; Children under 12 years of age half-price'. The return from Tenby was at seven in the evening.[150]

On 29 July 1844 about 450 members of the Swansea Oddfellows sailed on an excursion to Ilfracombe on board the *Lord Beresford* to meet members of the Bideford and Barnstaple Lodges for a dinner with speeches and songs. The outward voyage took three hours and the return three and a half. 'The only circumstance tending to mar the enjoyment of the day was the great sea-sickness which prevailed on board'.[151] (The *Lord Beresford* had been bought by Joseph Tregelles Price and started sailing on the Swansea to Bristol route in 1843.)

Some excursions were particularly unpleasant. Members of the Cardiff Oddfellows with wives and friends sailed on board the *Bristol* for a day excursion from the Bute Dock at Cardiff to Swansea on 29 June 1846. The weather was calm when they left at 7.00 a.m. However, when they reached Lavernock Point, about four miles out of Cardiff Bay, the ship had to turn to starboard into a south-west wind. 'Almost at the same moment the sea became deeply agitated, breaking over the vessel, which now laboured onwards, and rolled fearfully, and wetted all upon the foredeck. After a dreadfully tedious voyage – during which the gale increased to a storm, the sea ran high, washed over the vessel and completely drenched nearly every person on board' they reached the Mumbles about five miles west of Swansea having been at sea for nearly seven hours 'fagged almost to death, and completely worn out by having experienced sea-sickness of the most dreadful and debilitating kind'. They were told that if they wished to go to Swansea they would be landed at the Mumbles by boat. Then they would have to go to Swansea by omnibus or on foot. Those who did were 'most hospitably received' there. It was decided that the *Bristol* would stay at Swansea overnight and take those 'who were willing to trust themselves once more on board' to Cardiff on Tuesday. The ship left Swansea at eight in the morning. 'Nearly everyone suffered from the effects of sea-sickness until they reached Nash Point' when matters improved considerably. They reached Penarth Roads at half-past three and remained there at anchor until about eight in the evening when they were able to sail into Bute Dock.

There was no railway between Swansea and Cardiff in 1846 and those who were not prepared to sail back on the *Bristol* 'returned by mail and omnibus'. Relatives and friends at Cardiff had not received any news about the *Bristol* remaining overnight at Swansea 'and many were visited with the most dismal forebodings, actually believing that all had perished'. The newspaper report concluded with the comment that this experience 'will prove almost a death-blow to all future excursions of this nature, to Swansea, at least'.[152] However, this was not so and excursions on all routes increased in number.

On 27 July 1846 'a party of holiday-seekers proceeded from the village of Neath Abbey in a newly launched (screw) steam-packet to Tenby, and enjoyed themselves during the day in various ways. We understand that the steamer reflects great credit upon the skill and judgment of Mr. A. Sturge, under whose superintendence she was built'.[153] This newly launched steam packet was the *Neath Abbey*.

There is some information available about the cost of hiring a steamer for an excursion. In reports of the difficulty experienced by the Committee of the Cardiff Mechanics' Institute in arranging an excursion on 19 August 1845 for which they had attempted to book the *Lady Charlotte* of the Bristol Steam Navigation Company, they considered the possibility of hiring the *Prince of Wales* which Joseph Tregelles Price had offered to the Committee of the Wesleyan School for £15. His proposed charge to the Mechanics was £20.[154] In the event the Mechanics' Institute's excursion took place on 18 August on board the *Lady Charlotte*. In August 1852, the cost of hiring the *Neath Abbey* for an excursion from Aberavon to Ilfracombe was apparently £20.[155] (This excursion is described below.)

An action in the Swansea County Court for Breach of Contract in 1870 throws some light on the process of hiring a steamer, the cost and the financial risk involved. In June 1870 Mr. Poley, proprietor of the Swan Inn, Neath, made an agreement with J. W. Pockett of Swansea to hire the *Prince of Wales*, which Pockett now owned, for an excursion to Ilfracombe on 4 July for £18. On 1 July Poley informed Pockett that he could not pay for the vessel beforehand, as he had only sold £2 worth of tickets. Pockett replied that he would send the ship to Neath on Saturday, 2 July so that she would be ready for the excursion as arranged. On Monday morning Poley said that the weather was not suitable, and the excursion would not take place. Pockett said that it was blowing a breeze but not very strong and on the same day his other vessel, the *Velindra*, took a trip to Ilfracombe from Swansea. After some delay the captain sailed to Ilfracombe without passengers in order to fulfil another engagement to carry excursionists between ports on the North Devon coast but arrived too late. Pockett sued Poley to recover the sum of £18. Poley argued that he was not liable as the weather was too bad. However, the judge accepted Pockett's argument that it was an absolute contract which had been fully carried out and the weather had nothing to do with it. He gave judgement for the plaintiff for the amount claimed with costs.[156]

Excursionists brought welcome business to the places they visited as shown in this report of excursions to Ilfracombe in July 1848.

> It is pleasing to reflect on the change the power of steam is producing in the habits of society, for instead of spending their money and their time in the brutal sports of bye-gone days, the labouring classes are induced to take pleasure trips from one country to another, as is

manifest from the frequency of excursions from Swansea, Neath, and other places on the Welsh coast, to Ilfracombe during the present summer. On Monday last this town was enlivened and the inhabitants gratified by the arrival of the *Lord Beresford* steamer from Swansea, with upwards of 300 passengers, on a pleasure excursion; and about an hour after the *Neath Abbey* steamer, propelled by the Archimedian [*sic*], screw, arrived with her decks literally crowded with a pleasure party from Neath. The steamers had each a splendid brass band on board, and as they neared the harbour the music sounded over the water delightfully. As soon as the party landed, horses, donkeys, and vehicles of different descriptions, were in requisition to take them to the tea and fruit gardens at Heale [*sic*], where refreshment was provided according to previous arrangements. Later in the day the bands played some enlivening airs through the town, and the weather being extremely delightful, the inhabitants seemed to participate in the pleasure, and altogether the town presented the appearance of a gala day. About four o'clock the parties assembled to return again to the principality, all apparently well pleased with the day's recreation, and no doubt will often talk of the beauties of Ilfracombe and advise their friends and neighbours to accompany them on similar excursions next summer.[157]

Unfortunately, excursionists did not always behave themselves well. On 15 June 1852 the *Neath Abbey* sailed from Neath with two or three hundred passengers on a trip to Bideford. They left Neath at one o'clock in the morning and arrived in Barnstaple Bay after a very uncomfortable passage. Faced with 'a long line of roaring, obstreperous breakers' it was decided not to attempt to sail into Bideford and they sailed instead to Ilfracombe arriving:

in very good time to begin the day's diversions. The company were in a very sorry trim – ladies' lower extremities immersed half the way up the leg – but all sickness and sadness, moisture, and misery, soon disappeared amidst general hospitalities and under a warm sun. A smart band piped up the street […] and having piled instruments at the 'London Inn,' all betook themselves to their customary recreations. Donkeys had to run the usual gauntlet, but in this their purgatory was brief, as the company, so the tide would have it, had to be starting again at about two o'clock. Brief as was the period of their stay it was long enough for some sorry exhibitions of intemperance. One "*lady*" was so tipsy as scarcely to be able to keep her seat on the donkey, and two *boys* were seen in a state of intoxication steering their rambling way towards the vessel. When will people learn, if nothing more, to keep within the limits of public decency?'[158]

There was another excursion to Ilfracombe several weeks later:

"GOOD MASTERS MAKE GOOD SERVANTS," – On Saturday [28 August] an excursion extraordinary from our over-the-water neighbours made its appearance in our waters, blotting out the statement we made the week before that we had recorded the last visit for the season. The *Neath Abbey* steamer brought some three or four hundred souls, consisting chiefly of the men belonging to some considerable works at Aberavon, with their wives and families. Their employers bore the entire expense of their holiday. It was not with them a simple permission to leave their work, but they hired a steamer for the purpose of conveying them to Ilfracombe, at an expense it is said, of some 20 pounds, paid the men their wages as if they had been at work, and also gave them a breakfast and dinner. That no sense might want its appropriate gratification a band of music was in attendance to charm with its notes their passage across and presence here. They engaged in their usual pastimes, and returned at an early hour in the afternoon, ready, no doubt, to repay by willing and grateful service the kind treatment of their chiefs. Other parties willing to join the trip were allowed to do so at a shilling a-head [*sic*]. The presence of the Welsh, the numerous visitors, with the usual influx on a market day filled our streets on Saturday with an unusual amount of business and bustle.[159]

The 'considerable works' referred to were probably the Cwmavon Works of the English Copper Company which was celebrating the renewal of its Charter in 1852 after four years of dispute during which the works were under the control of the Bank of England as mortgagees in possession.[160]

During early 1853 there was concern at Ilfracombe that there would be no summer excursions from Wales because 'the Government had, to prevent danger, forbidden steamers carrying such a number of passengers as were necessary to "pay the way" on such occasions. The way things have gone this Summer seemed to justify that report, until last Monday [11 July], when to the great joy of fruit sellers, donkey drivers, and houses of entertainment, there appeared in our waters the steamer *Neath Abbey* from Neath, with a cargo of about 100 of the southern Cymri [*sic*]. […] After going through the usual exercises on these trips of pleasure, the party returned, like good and orderly citizens, to the land of metal and coal'.¹⁶¹

There are two contrasting reports of an excursion from Neath to Ilfracombe on 16 July 1855. First, the English report:

> OUR WELSH FRIENDS. – On Monday our harbour had quite an important appearance, having no less than *four* steamers – more than ever met there before at one time. There was the *Juno*, whose weekly trips have contributed so largely to fill the lodging houses, waiting to sail for Bristol – the *Lord Beresford*, on her usual trading trip from Swansea, and two "excursion" steamers – the *Neath Abbey*, from Neath, and the *Jenny Jones*, from Cardiff. These last brought over nearly 500 holiday folk from the Principality, the presence of dog-days, and the ripe strawberries reminding them of their favourite resort. The pouring on shore of this half-thousand pleasure seekers with their bands and bustle, and the turning out of the inhabitants to greet and gaze, gave the town quite a holiday aspect. What with the unusual number of lodgers, this large accession from the land beyond, and parties coming in from the country to meet their friends, some people thought there never was so large a population on the ground at one time before. The day turned out fine, notwithstanding the unpromising morning, and those who came for pleasure were able to take it. The crowd soon dispersed itself into the streets and about the promenades, the donkeys were all in requisition, a numerous party betaking themselves to the tea-gardens at Hele. About four o'clock, the tide, which had been, notwithstanding the excitement, proceeding very coolly with its part of the business, gave the note of departure, and for the next hour and half the quay presented a very animated and interesting scene. The *Juno* was the first to haul out, then the *Neath Abbey*, with her 250 souls, after her the *Jenny Jones*, and last of all the *Beresford*. By half-past five the whole had cleared out, and were on their watery way for their homes and homely life.¹⁶²

By contrast, the *Welshman* reported:

> The weather was very unfavourable, but the prices of 3s. for best cabin, and 2s. for the second, must have offered an inducement, as considerable [*sic*] more than 200 persons went by it, and at least 50 more applications were refused for want of room.¹⁶³

On 30 July 1855 there was another trip from Neath to Ilfracombe:

> OUR NEVER-FAILING VISITORS. – The men of the Principality – and the women, too – evidently know what is good for themselves, and think they can't have too much of a good thing. Two "Excursions" came on Monday, numbering about 400 souls – 300 from Swansea by the *Lord Beresford*, and 100 from Neath, by the *Neath Abbey*. They landed about half-past eight in the morning, accompanied by their bands, and welcomed by crowds of people on the quay. The weather was not exactly what holiday people desire; they, nevertheless, contrived to enjoy themselves after the usual fashion, keeping the town alive in all directions. In the afternoon, from three to half-past four the quay was thronged; first, the *Juno* moved off, taking away a greater number than people wished to see depart just now; next came the *Neath Abbey*, with its quota; and last, the *Beresford*, with more people than she brought, besides cattle and cargo. Gaily they steamed away to the land of the mountain and the mine.[164]

On 12 May 1856, there was an excursion by the *Neath Abbey* from Bristol to Flat Holm where a large number of passengers went ashore. One of them, a sailmaker from Bristol, Charles Evans, decided to swim. He ignored warnings from his friends, stripped off his clothes apart from his shirt, plunged into the water, swam strongly at first but was carried away by the current and sank. Boats were manned but to no avail.[165]

Perhaps the following report of excursions to Ilfracombe in June 1856 hints that the people of Ilfracombe found visitors from the English side of the Channel more to their liking.

> The usual summer visits from various places on both sides of the Channel to this attractive locality have commenced. The *Neath Abbey* has brought two large parties this week, the first was from Neath, and amounted to about 140 persons. They brought a band with them, and, after enjoying themselves for half-a-dozen hours, departed peacefully to their homes. The Monday [23 June] party was from Watchet, consisting of about 110 persons. They were particularly noticed by the natives as a very respectable, well-dressed, and well-conducted party, who appeared to be well-pleased with what they saw. The steamer returned about half-past five.[166]

The *Neath Abbey* took about 300 holiday people 'from the Welsh side' to

Ilfracombe on 16 August, 1856. 'After enjoying themselves for the usual time, between the morning and the evening tides, [they] steamed off about five o'clock to the music of their excellent band. Being market day, these visitors became extensive customers in the pannier market, and soon cleared what was to be sold'.[167]

Sometimes tragedy struck on an excursion as in the case of the trip to Flat Holm in May 1856. A far worse tragedy occurred in June 1859 when the *Neath Abbey* was chartered to take an excursion from Bristol to Watchet and Minehead. All the arrangements were the responsibility of the organisers of the excursion. The *Neath Abbey* sailed to Watchet and Minehead on Whit Monday, 13 June, returning to pick up passengers on the Tuesday. On that day, after picking up the passengers at Minehead, she anchored about half a mile off the pier at Watchet. 'The boats employed to bring the passengers from shore were too few for the number waiting and additional boats were engaged, including a boat belonging to the smack *Tom* which was 11 ft. long and 4ft 8 in wide and meant to carry 6 to 8 people. This boat put off from the shore with 13 people. Half way to the *Neath Abbey*, with the tide coming in and a ground swell, a large wave hit the boat swamping it and all the occupants went into the water. Another boat managed to pick up some of them but six people were drowned'.[168]

The Inquest was held at the Bell Inn, Watchet. Evidence having been given by several witnesses, the Coroner summed up saying:

> It had been clearly proved that the unfortunate results had occurred from the boat being overladen, thirteen passengers having been crowded into it, whereas it was only capable of carrying eight. The boat was commanded by George Wedlake and Alfred Short, who were the responsible parties, and the question for the jury was, whether they used due caution, in the discharge of their duties, in permitting so many passengers to get into the boat. It had been stated that the people rushed to the boat in a venturesome manner, and some were tipsy; still the parties in command of the boat were not bound to proceed with it if they considered it unsafe. It appeared, too, that the boat was a common punt, and, according to the evidence not more than eight persons ought to have entered it. After a lengthened deliberation the jury returned a verdict of "Manslaughter against George Wedlake and Alfred Short." The Coroner admitted the prisoners to bail, under the new act of parliament, on entering into two sureties each of £25, and their own recognizances of £50.[169]

On 9 August the Grand Jury at the Somerset Assizes found that there was insufficient evidence to establish that a crime had been committed and Wedlake and Short were discharged.[170]

Captain John Westlake of the *Neath Abbey* wrote a letter to the *Cardiff and Merthyr Guardian* 'in explanation of the circumstances attending the recent lamentable occurrence'. In it he stated:

> When we reached Watchet from Minehead, on Tuesday afternoon, I brought the steamer up as near to the rocks as it was safe to do, and in 10 feet of water, as indicated by the lead. After the tide had flowed a foot or two, we hove short the anchor, and dragged up nearer the shore, until hindered by a ridge of stones and the fishing stakes, close under our stern. The passengers were then beginning to come on board. I looked over our stern (we were then not a quarter of a mile from the shore), when I perceived a boat with passengers, very deeply laden. I kept looking at her; and, observing her to be fast settling down, I immediately jumped into our boat, with the mate, to go to the rescue; but by that time more of my crew had got into the boat, and at once pulled to the sinking one, and succeeded in saving the lives of nine men and one woman; and by that time the boat from the *Tom* had upset; ours at once pulled to her, and picked up two of her passengers, who were landed. In order to secure the safety of the boats which followed we passed all the lines we had on board, and attached cork 'fenders' to them to drift towards the boats, so that they might be hauled to the steamer, and this, doubtless prevented more loss of life'.[171]

Tenby was a very popular day trip destination. On Monday 11 August 1862, the *Neath Abbey* and the *Sampson* arrived from Neath and Llanelli; the *Sampson* was back again on Tuesday as well as the *President*, possibly from Carmarthen or Llanelli, and on Wednesday the *President* sailed into Tenby once more. 'On each occasion they were attended by brass bands, who headed the excursionists, when going from and to the vessels'.[172]

On 17 August 1863 the *Neath Abbey* set sail on an excursion from Neath to Ilfracombe but because of the exceedingly rough weather she was unable to cross the Channel and was driven into the Mumbles where the passengers went ashore. One of the passengers, James Jones, a boilersmith from Neath, who had never been to the Mumbles before, started picking up oysters and was attacked by a local Mumbles oyster merchant, Alexander Fleming. Jones suffered a severe wound to his head. The County Magistrates committed

Fleming for trial. At the Glamorganshire Sessions on 20 October Fleming was charged with cutting and wounding Jones and doing him grievous bodily harm. After hearing a portion of the evidence, the prosecuting lawyer threw up the case, and Fleming, who had borne a good character for many years, was discharged.[173]

It is notable that reports in Welsh newspapers of excursions from South Wales do not mention the behaviour of the excursionists but concentrate on their enjoyment and the weather but, as already noted, reports in English newspapers often comment frankly on the behaviour of visitors.

A report of an excursion to Ilfracombe on 20 July 1863 commented as follows:

> WELSH EXCURSIONISTS – On Monday last the steamers, the *Prince of Wales* and the *Neath Abbey* arrived here, crowded with living freights. After landing, about six hundred, nearly all of the working class, took possession of our streets. That poor ill-used quadruped, the donkey, came in for his share of whacks and kicks from the brutish "bipeds" that bestrode them. "Taffy" imbibed his favourite beverage – beer, and about four o'clock "made tracks" for the harbour, and as the wind was blowing dead against him, he had to make divers "tacks" to reach the steamer intended to convey them to the land of "leeks" and "hats." We have been favoured of late with many highly respectable excursions from Swansea and elsewhere, and at this season of the year it is most important our town should be the reverse of noise of brawling. Our opposite neighbours will be good enough to take the hint'.[174]

The 1864 season's first batch of excursionists, 'an unusually large number' visited Ilfracombe on 18 May from Swansea on board the *Prince of Wales*. 'They appeared to consist, for the most part, of the well-to-do folks of Swansea, and were therefore quite different to those who come from the iron and coal districts, and who astonish the people of Ilfracombe, by their enormous eating and drinking capabilities'. On 23 and 25 July 'large numbers of people from Neath and Swansea arrived here [Ilfracombe] by excursion steamers. They consisted almost entirely of the men employed in the collieries and foundries of those places; and, if drinking and donkey-riding constitute enjoyment, they must have thoroughly enjoyed themselves'.[175]

An interesting commentary on the behaviour of many excursionists appeared in the report of 'a gigantic excursion' from Port Talbot to Ilfracombe on 20 August 1864 in which men employed in the iron works of Cwmavon and Taibach numbering 'with the females' about 750 people,' and accompanied by the 9th Glamorgan Rifles Volunteer Band, sailed on the *Prince of Wales* and the *Henry Southan*.[176] After commenting on a morning concert given by the band at the Town Hall when 'the music; both vocal and instrumental was extremely good,' the report continued:

> 'Seldom has a rougher lot of excursionists visited Ilfracombe than those of Saturday. I do not mean rough only in appearance, but in manner and conduct. The great majority of them, both men and women, became drunk before leaving; and by their noise and violence created quite a stir. One of them strongly evinced the contempt in which he held the principles of the Society for the Prevention of Cruelty to Animals, by hammering a poor donkey, much in the same way as he would a sheet of copper, for which humane exercise he was placed in "durance vile" until the boat left in the evening. Another, whose genius was more under the control of self-interest, determined to secure a memento of his visit to Ilfracombe in the shape of a purloined umbrella, and he was successful. A compatriot, of similar bent, was detected in the very act of bearing off a cane, to which of course he had no right. These little harmless displays of Welsh eccentricity were varied by a fight or two, which issued in the breaking of a window, and of course enhanced the interest of the day's proceedings.

However, the writer qualified his criticism.

> The men who work in the iron and copper works of Wales earn, as a rule, good wages and spend their money freely and foolishly. Although they form a large proportion of the inhabitants of the iron and coal districts, they are by no means to be taken as fair representatives of the Welsh working class, either in appearance or manners. They are altogether exceptional to the general state of things. Placed in one of the hardest conditions of human life, deprived of many of its amenities, and subject to most of its accidents, it is no wonder that they are a rude, rough set of men. The dangerous, arduous nature of their employment may be seen in the appearance of the men themselves. From the rapid alternations of the heat and cold to which they are constantly exposed, the countenances of even the youngest, soon become wan and sallow; the cheek, pallid; the eyes sunken, and the whole appearance, emaciated and cadaverous; and from the many accidents to which they are liable, it is a common thing to see an eye or finger gone, a leg or arm crushed

by the machinery. The old men among them, in some cases, bear as many scars as the soldier of many fights. The ordinary pastime of these men's lives is made up of working, eating, and, in a less degree, of sleeping; and, had they inclination, they have scarcely time for any self-improvement. I am not constituting myself the apologist for these rude men, but merely stating the facts of their position which are such as not to lead to the expectation of anything very refined.

After a description of the iron and copper works and working conditions, he concluded:

Such are the men, and such their employment, who form the greatest part of all the excursions that visit us from Wales. The amount of money they leave behind them more than counterbalances any little annoyance they may cause.

There was a very bad storm in the Neath area on 16 June 1866 as the following report describes:

The weather, after several weeks being fine and dry, has, during the past week, been of a very changeable, and at times an exceedingly boisterous character. On Saturday evening last, between nine and ten o'clock, a very severe squall, accompanied by thunder and lightning, suddenly sprang up from the S.S.W., doing considerable damage to trees, roofs of houses, and demolishing buildings in the neighbourhood. On the same evening the *Neath Abbey*, steamer, which was returning from an excursion from Neath to Ilfracombe, encountered some very rough weather, by which many of the passengers suffered from sea-sickness, and became greatly alarmed, but, through the skilful and experienced management of Captain Westlake, all were safely landed at Neath.[177]

Under the title of 'The Last of the Season,' a pleasure trip was arranged for Saturday, 3 August 1867 on board the *Neath Abbey*, leaving the Neath wharf early on Saturday morning for Tenby, and returning 'in time for the evening's tide, so that late hours and a day's pleasure will not for once go hand-in-hand'. The 'attraction of the band of the 17th Glamorgan Rifle Volunteers [was] also offered as an inducement to the votaries of Terpsichore'. The vessel was said to have been chartered by the band. After the event it was reported that the 'excursion was one of the pleasantest of the season, and the weather being delightfully fine, the enjoyment was without any "disagreeables." […] The band "discoursed sweet music" in their usual excellent style, and the votaries of Terpsichore had their fill of dancing both on shore and afloat. The entire arrangements were excellent, and beyond question admirably carried out'.[178]

On 3 July 1871 there were two marine excursions to Ilfracombe, one by the *Prince of Wales* from Cardiff and the other by the *Neath Abbey* from Neath. It was reported that 'no accident happened, but the boisterous state of the weather had a very serious effect upon a large number of the excursionists, whose constitutions were ill-adapted for a trip across the channel'.[179]

During the period of operation between Bristol and Bideford or Barnstaple the *Neath Abbey* ran many excursions along the Somerset and Devon coast.

On 8 June 1875, a week after commencing the Bristol to Bideford service, 'Capt. Clibbett, commander of the *Neath Abbey*, took a very large party on a moon-light trip. The party went from Bideford Bay, past Spratridge [*sic*] Buoy, and as far as Hartland Point. A band was on board, and a most enjoyable evening spent'.[180]

There was a day excursion from Bideford to Lundy Island on 4 August 1875 calling at Clovelly with the times of departure and return arranged to link with trains from and to Barnstaple and elsewhere and allowing five hours on Lundy.[181]

The ship was advertised to leave Bideford Quay at 7.30 a.m., calling off Appledore and Instow at 8.00, and returning from Lundy at 3.30 and Clovelly at 4.30, arriving at Instow and Bideford in time for trains leaving for Barnstaple and Torrington. Fares from Bideford to Lundy and back were Cabin 3s. 6d. and Fore Deck 2s. 6d. and one shilling less for Bideford to Clovelly and back. 'Refreshments to be had on board at moderate charges. A first-class band will be in attendance.' On 5 August it was reported that 'long before the advertised time for sailing, there was a tremendous rush to the steamer, and scores who had come from long distances, as well as many in the town, were left behind'.[182]

Two more excursions to Lundy Island were arranged in the same month, one from Bideford and Westward Ho! on 18 August with six hours on the Island, and the other from Barnstaple on 19 August, calling at Instow and Appledore, with five hours on Lundy, both leaving at 7.30 in the morning. The excursion on 18 August 'was in every way satisfactory' except that the *Neath Abbey* left Bideford with not more than 60 people on board.[183]

Unfortunately, the trip from Barnstaple on 19 August did not go according to plan. The ship had 'not gone many yards before she grounded on a sand ridge'. Passengers aboard had to land in boats and those waiting to board at Instow and Appledore waited in vain. Newspapers blamed the pilot. There was much speculation and controversy locally. The *North Devon Journal* claimed that the trip was under the auspices of the Good Templars, a temperance society advocating total abstinence, and stated that there was speculation about whether the ship was grounded by accident or design. It also claimed that the ship was 'so firmly wedged in the sand that they had trouble before she could be backed off on the evening's tide'. It was even suggested by some that the grounding was a deliberate act by Joseph Stribling, Sen., the pilot, who, it was alleged, had been bribed 'by some parties of the town' with a sovereign to run her ashore and the promise of another if done well. There appear to have been reports of bad behaviour by some of the passengers. Mr. Heaven, the owner of Lundy Island, wrote a letter, published in the *North Devon Herald*, in which comments were made that their behaviour was 'a disgust and a disgrace'.

George B. Pearse, Agent for the *Neath Abbey* at Barnstaple, dealt with these accusations in letters to the *North Devon Journal*. He wrote that the ship had been delayed in leaving Barnstaple because he kept the boat waiting for passengers after it was high water and as a result there was 'over a foot ebb on leaving the Quay'; there was no truth in the bribery rumour and the grounding was not done wilfully but was an error of judgment; 'the company on board would have been a credit for anyone to have introduced to that gentleman on whose property they would have been landed had all went well, and not a disgust and a disgrace as a great many of those were reported to have been by Mr. Heaven's letter;' there was no difficulty in getting the ship off the sandbank on the following tide. Furthermore, the excursion was not under the auspices of the Good Templars. 'None but myself had anything to do with it, and [the *Neath Abbey*] was allowed to come here by her proprietor for our Barnstaple people to have an excursion by her to the island; and, furthermore, for our tradesmen to see by what they were having their goods in'. In a footnote to his letter published on 26 August, in which he dealt with the accusation of deliberate stranding as a result of bribery, Pearse wrote that 'It is said to have been a drunken frolic and done out of a spleen against me'. He was the Harbourmaster at Barnstaple as well as acting as Agent there for the *Neath Abbey*. It is possible that in either of these capacities he had alienated some local interest. Later reports do not suggest any further problems.[184]

On the evening of 23 June 1876 the *Neath Abbey* made her first excursion trip of the season from Bideford. 'The weather was delightful and the trip very much enjoyed'. According to this brief report it was intended to have a succession of excursion trips during the season. I have not found any information of them.[185]

In July 1877 it was reported that the *Neath Abbey* would 'afford the inhabitants of Barnstaple the opportunity of a trip to Lundy Island on Saturday, 28 July. If only the weather be fine, we have no doubt numbers will be glad to enjoy the pleasant marine excursion. She will call off Appledore and Instow both going and returning'. The fares were 3s. 6d. for the After Cabin and 2s. 6d. for the Fore Cabin. Refreshments would be available. The ship would leave Barnstaple Quay at 7.30 a.m. and depart from Lundy at 4.00 p.m. The advertisement in the same paper included:

> CAUTION. – As damage has hitherto been done by Excursionists on the Island, together with gross misconduct, the Proprietor is fully determined in future to prosecute all parties committing such like offences, the party in whose charge the Excursion is being answerable to him for good conduct.[186]

In the event the excursionists behaved very well on the Island.

> The morning was not very promising, but, by a quarter to eight, when the vessel left the quay, about one hundred and thirty were on board, and, after she had taken her departure, not a few came to the starting point and found themselves too late. The *Neath Abbey* called at Instow and Appledore on her voyage, and received fresh excursionists at each point. She reached Lundy about half-past eleven, and landed her passengers, who enjoyed themselves on the island until a quarter to five, when steam was again got up to return. Shortly after eight the neat little craft reached Barnstaple Quay, and those on board expressed themselves highly pleased with their day's outing. The excursionists, by their conduct, fully justified the confidence which Mr. G. B. Pearce [*sic*] expressed when he obtained Mr. W. H. Heaven's permission to land on the island.[187]

On 1 August H. G. Heaven, the son of W. H. Heaven, wrote to G. B. Pearse as follows:

> I think it right to send you a line to say that, with one exception, your excursionists, on Saturday, gave us no cause for complaint. The one exception was that they left the gates open between the fields, by which the stock was let run into the standing corn, doing considerable

damage, to the amount of some £20. Excursionists ought to be careful equally to abstain from wilful damage and careless damage. The latter is often more serious than the former, and it is too bad for persons, from sheer carelessness and laziness, to expose us to so much damage. Had we not discovered the missing bullocks two hours after the steamer left, thirty acres of good corn might have been irretrievably ruined, as some thirty or forty head of cattle had found their way in. If you could let this be known amongst any excursionists, past or future, it may prevent anything of the sort again.

The letter was published in the *North Devon Herald* at the request of Mr. Pearse.[188]

The running of excursions by steam packet boats such as the *Neath Abbey* became less frequent for two reasons. The development of railways resulted in railway companies offering a wide range of excursions from a multiplicity of local stations in South Wales and the West Country. More significantly, 'pleasure steamers' were introduced on the Bristol Channel, ships designed to carry passengers only and with more attractive on-board facilities. The first of these is considered to have been the *Lyn*, built at Glasgow in 1878 for running between Portishead and Ilfracombe. 'She had a promenade deck, 128 ft. long, a "smoking deck" of 28 ft., first and second class saloons and dining room'.[189] During the 1880s the number of passenger-only ships on the Bristol Channel increased significantly. By 1888 the Scottish business of P. & A. Campbell had begun operating from Bristol and made that city its headquarters in 1889.[190] Although steam packets continued to run some excursions that business was gradually taken over by the pleasure steamers. In the meanwhile, the *Neath Abbey* had ceased to run a packet service from Neath to Bristol in November 1887 and when she started sailing again in August 1890 from Swansea to Bristol it was as a freight-only service.

CHAPTER 8

Evan Evans's Personal Use of the *Neath Abbey*

From time to time Evan Evans used the *Neath Abbey* in connection with other interests of his and occasionally he also used the vessel as his private yacht.

In 1859, because of the perceived threat of invasion from France, the establishment of volunteer rifle corps was permitted by the British government and in 1860 the 17th Glamorgan Rifle Volunteers were set up. The corps was raised by Evan Evans who was commissioned Captain with his son-in-law David Bevan as lieutenant. A company of about 100 was raised, mainly from brewery workers. The corps was equipped and maintained largely by Evan Evans at his own expense.[191]

On 17 June 1862 a Grand Review of Volunteer Corps was held at Durdham Down, Bristol, with volunteer regiments from a substantial part of England and South Wales. Before the event it was reported that:

> The Vale of Neath Rifles, 100 strong, a corps which has been fully equipped and maintained at an expense of some thousands of pounds by their gallant commander, Captain Evan Evans, of the Neath brewery, will arrive in Bristol on the day preceding the review, in the *Neath Abbey* steamer, which belongs to Captain Evan Evans, and will return on Wednesday. This liberal gentleman has deputed a friend in Bristol to engage beds for the whole of his corps on Monday and Tuesday nights, and has undertaken to defray the whole of the expense attending their three days' visit to Bristol.[192]

The men were inspected in full uniform at their Cadoxton, Neath, headquarters on Saturday afternoon, 14 June.

> On Monday morning about eight o'clock the company again met on the Neath Quay, pursuant to arrangements, and shortly after proceeded

to embark on board the *Neath Abbey* steamer (the property of their captain, E. Evans, Esq.) for the purpose of taking part in the grand review at Bristol. The whole of the company were soon on board, and everything being in readiness the *Neath Abbey* let go and steamed away, to the strains of their excellent band, amid the cheers of those on shore.[193]

During the Review 'at about half-past twelve, the Neath Rifles (the 17th Glamorgan) put in an appearance, headed by their band, and marched to the part of the field assigned to the second battalion. They were a fine body of men, and attracted considerable attention'.[194]

On Wednesday, 31 July 1867, the Seventh Annual Review of the Glamorganshire Volunteers was held on the Crymlyn Burrows, on the right bank of the River Neath, and was watched by not less than 15,000 people. It was reported that 'Captain Evans's *Neath Abbey* steamer lay high and dry on the beach, covered with gay bunting, and made unmistakeable efforts to assist in the day's proceedings'.[195]

While Evan Evans was away 'on his customary tour,' in late summer 1860, the corps and some of their friends decided to present him with 'a sword and appendages' on his return. The sum of £50 was raised. Mr Rayner, a silversmith of Swansea, supplied 'a splendid sword of Damascus steel, silver scabbard, beautifully embossed silver hilt and guard, silver rings and buckles, shoulder and waist belt profusely ornamented with silver, silver chain, and a handsome shako also ornamented with silver lace and surmounted with a plume of cock's feathers.' The presentation was delayed until the afternoon of 19 November. It took place at Cadoxton, in a field adjoining Evan Evans's house, Cadoxton Lodge. In responding Captain Evans said that:

> at the latter end of the summer, he visited the coast of France. He started from Jersey, where he was staying, taking a French pilot in his steamer, and visited Cherbourg. After due observance of the requirements that foreigners should go under the stern of the Admiral's ship, they took up a position in the anchorage ground, and in the course of the day the captain and himself went on shore. He made some enquiries about the Government Dockyard, for the purpose of getting over it, but he was informed that there were many difficulties in the way; but he was not to be daunted, and accordingly went to the British Consul; there he met with no better success, for he was told by the Consul that he had written a great many notes for persons who were

very anxious to go over the docks, and they had all failed. He (Capt. Evans) then determined to go to the Admiral of the port. Some questions were asked him by the Admiral, and as he spoke English they became pretty familiar, and he gave him an order to go over the Dockyard. He also showed him the room in which Her Majesty had some refreshment when she was at Cherbourg, and altogether he was treated in the most courteous manner by the French authorities. They appeared to be very kindly disposed towards this country; and it was for those reasons that he hoped that peace would long continue between the two greatest nations in the world.[196]

The tour took place in September. A 'Notice to Shippers' was published by the Agents, Thomas & Son, Bristol, and J. L. Matthews, Neath, stating that the '*Neath Abbey* Steamer being off the Station for a short time, Sailing Vessels will take in Goods regularly until the Steamer resumes'.[197] She was back on Station by mid-September as a report of her arriving at Padstow on 14 September shows.[198] John Westlake was master at this time.

In July 1867 Evan Evans took a party of friends on board the *Neath Abbey* to visit Spithead, where a Naval Review attended by the Sultan of Turkey took place on 17 July, as well as the Isle of Wight and other places. On 10 August the *Swansea and Glamorgan Herald* reported that our 'interesting report of the presence of the *Neath Abbey* steamer with Captain Evans and his friends, at Spithead […] is unavoidably postponed till next week'. Unfortunately, that report does not appear to have been published. It was reported that the *Neath Abbey* left Plymouth for Portsmouth on 16 July and left Dartmouth for Plymouth on 28 July.[199] Evan Evans was a member and treasurer of Zoar Chapel, Neath, and a report of the annual Tea Meeting held on 1 August commented that Captain Evan's 'marine excursion to Spithead, &c., has evidently done his health no injury'.[200]

CHAPTER 9

Goods Traffic and the Coming of Railways

Although built to carry passengers as well as cargo, the *Neath Abbey* was essentially a hard-working cargo carrier between Bristol Channel ports. She also carried animals. In August 1846 the charges were dogs 2s. 6d., pigs 1s. 6d. and sheep 1s.[201] The range of charges was extended in January 1847 with charges for horses at 12s. 6d., and cattle 7s. 6d. The charge for a dog was reduced to 2s.[202] Charges for horses and cattle were reduced to 10s. and 6s. respectively in September 1871.[203]

The cargoes carried varied. Very often newspaper reports of her departures and arrivals simply mention 'general cargo' or 'sundries,' terms referring to mixed cargoes when carried on those voyages, but there are frequent mentions of cargoes of iron, copper, copper ore, lead, coal, flour, maize, wheat or barley. After linking with the railway companies, it was advertised that the ship carried 'every description of merchandise traffic'.

Warehouse facilities were provided at Neath from the inception of the service in 1846 and from 1 April 1861 it was advertised that 'Goods for Briton Ferry will be Discharged into a Warehouse solely for that purpose near the Ferry'.[204]

On 28 September 1877 the *Neath Abbey* sailed from Briton Ferry for Bristol but 'put back for a quantity of tinplate'.[205] This is the first mention I have found of tinplate as a cargo on her although she must have carried tinplate on many previous occasions given the significant expansion of tinplate manufacturing in the area between Port Talbot and Llanelli in the late 1860s and especially in the 1870s. From then on tin or tinplate is the most frequently identified cargo.

Although not mentioned it is assumed that special arrangements existed for the carriage of coffins. On 22 March 1871 the remains of Mr. William Rendell, a chemist at Briton Ferry, who had died of congestion of the lungs at the age of 32, 'were embarked upon the *Neath Abbey* steamer [...] for Bristol, *en route* to Taunton, in Somersetshire'.[206] In 1875 the body of Captain Daniel Walters, owner and master of the *Ann*, was taken to his home port of Bideford on board the *Neath Abbey*.[207] The death of Captain Walters, whose body was found in the Basin at Bristol on 26 May 1875, has already been mentioned in Chapter 5.

The *Neath Abbey* started her career on the Bristol Channel in 1846, just before a period of substantial railway development that revolutionised goods and passenger traffic within South and Mid-Wales, and with England.

In 1846 the only proper railway in South Wales, as distinct from private industrial tramways linking iron works or collieries to each other and to canals, was the Taff Vale Railway, opened in 1840/1841, and that line only ran between Cardiff and Merthyr. The Oystermouth Railway, later known as the Swansea and Mumbles Railway, was a horse-drawn tramway carrying some goods traffic such as limestone in its early days. It began carrying passengers in 1807 but it did not do so between 1826/1827 and about 1860 and the line was derelict for much of that time.[208]

The most important and effective means of communication with England was provided by shipping on the Bristol Channel and Bristol was of enormous commercial importance to South Wales. In spite of the subsequent development of the railway network the Bristol Channel remained a vital means of communication between South Wales and Bristol and the West Country for most of the nineteenth century for passengers and continued longer for freight, with the cross-channel steamers providing convenient links with railways in South Wales.

The South Wales Railway opened from Chepstow to Swansea via Neath on 18 June 1850. On 23 September 1851 the Vale of Neath Railway opened from Neath to Hirwaun and Aberdare. The opportunity railway development provided for the steamship business to offer through carriage of goods to inland locations was recognised very quickly.

> It is expected that a huge quantity of goods from Bristol, for Brecon and other districts, will be brought by the *Neath Abbey* steamer, to Neath, and thence per the Vale of Neath Railway to Hirwain, from which place they will [...] be forwarded the same day by waggon, and be delivered at their destination the second day after leaving Bristol, which will be a saving of several days, instead of forwarding them by the canal from Newport, according to the old system.[209]

'The canal from Newport' was the Monmouthshire Canal from Newport to a junction with the Brecon & Abergavenny Canal and on to Brecon.

This established the pattern for extending faster through carriage of goods from Bristol via Neath to many inland towns and villages in South and Mid-Wales as the railway network developed over the years. The Vale of Neath line was extended from Hirwaun to Merthyr in October 1853 and from Neath to Swansea (the Swansea and Neath Railway) in 1863. The Neath & Brecon Railway opened from Neath to Onllwyn at the head of the Dulais Valley in September 1864 and reached Brecon in June 1867. The Brecon and Merthyr line opened to Dowlais in 1863 and to Merthyr in 1868. The Mid-Wales Railway connecting Llanidloes to a link with the Brecon and Merthyr Railway at Talyllyn Junction, 4 miles east of Brecon, opened in 1864. From the end of 1873 the Swansea Vale and Neath & Brecon Junction Railway linked the Swansea Vale Railway with the Neath & Brecon by means of a line seven miles long from Ynysgeinon Junction, near Ystalyfera, twelve miles from Swansea on the former, to Colbren Junction, one mile from Onllwyn on the latter.[210]

The Vale of Neath Railway Station was originally located very near to the existing Neath Railway Station but in 1863 the Vale of Neath started using the Swansea to Neath Railway station, known as Neath Low Level, located close to the western end of the Neath River Bridge, just a short walk from the Town Quay at the eastern end of the bridge and the Neath Abbey Packet Wharf a little downstream from there. The Neath & Brecon also used this station as its terminus. The result was that goods brought from Bristol by the *Neath Abbey* could be transhipped at Neath Low Level Station onto the Vale of Neath Railway or, from 1864, the Neath and Brecon Railway.

The steamship company arranged reduced through rates with these railway companies and over the years the advertisements for the *Neath Abbey* show an expanding list of destinations.

The first advertisement appears to have been at the beginning of 1852:

Steam Communication between Bristol and Neath and thence per Vale of Neath and South Wales Railways to Aberdare, Hirwain, Glyn-Neath, Aberavon, Cwmavon, Maesteg, and places adjacent.[211]

By May 1867 the advertisement was for:

Direct Communication between Bristol and Stations on the Neath & Brecon and Mid-Wales Railways, for every description of Merchandise Traffic.

The Public are respectfully informed that the Proprietor of the *Neath Abbey* screw Steamship has made arrangements for through Rates with the Neath and Brecon and Mid-Wales Railways, and Goods are now Carried by this route from Bristol, to the following places, at considerably reduced Charges, viz:– Crynant, Onllwyn, Penwyllt, Devynock, Senny Bridge, Trecastle, Brecon, Trefeinon, Talgarth, Boughrood, Erwood, Builth, Newbridge-on-Wye, Doldenlod, Rhayader-Pantydwr, Tylwch, Llanidloes, and places adjacent.[212]

The poster mentioned in the Foreword which advertises the *Neath Abbey* service for December 1870 provides more information, including the ship's schedule and fares, and it names a different selection of stations served, omitting mid-Wales stations but including stations served by the Vale of Neath Railway and the Swansea Vale Railway.[213] It should be noted that the illustration of a ship on that and similar posters as well as in newspaper advertisements was not intended to be a representation of the ship featured but was a generic representation of the type of ship. The poster is shown in Illustration 7 on page 67.

In 1861 there was great dissatisfaction in Maesteg and district about the charges levied by the Llynvi Valley Railway Company to take goods up to Maesteg from the South Wales Railway Company station at Bridgend. It was reported that a 'respectable commercial traveller from Bristol, who is doing extensive business in Maesteg, says that every order which he has received this journey has been accompanied with the strictest injunction from those who gave it, to forward their goods via the *Neath Abbey* steamer, instead of per rail'.[214]

An example of the complexity of through carriage of goods, albeit one that did not end happily, is provided by the case of *Thomas Evans, of Aberaman* v. *The Vale of Neath Railway Company* heard at Merthyr County Court on 12 January 1854.

In October 1853 a hogshead of molasses was sent from Bristol to the plaintiff, addressed to 'Mr. Thos. Evans, per *Neath Abbey* and *Vale of Neath Rail*.' At Neath the hogshead was transferred from the ship to the Vale of Neath Railway Company and carried by train to Aberdare station where it was handed over to a carrier, Ebenezer Davies, who was not in the company's employ. In taking down the hogshead from the van, Davies let it fall and the damage caused the loss of about a quarter of its contents. He gave Evans the bill which Evans refused to sign.

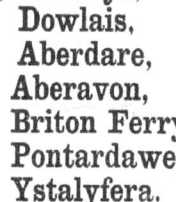

ILLUSTRATION 7
Poster for Neath to Bristol Service December 1870.

The railway company suggested unsuccessfully that the plaintiff should have brought his action against the packet company or against the carrier, Davies. They argued that Davies was not a railway company servant but an independent carrier. However, the evidence showed that, although Davies had a cart and wagon of his own, the van in which he delivered the molasses to the plaintiff's house had the name of the railway company on it, he had with him the company's delivery book, the bill given to the plaintiff on the 11th of October declared, 'Mr. Evans, debtor to the Vale of Neath Railway Company;' and the bill included the railway company charge of 1s. 10d. for delivery. The judge decided that Davies had not delivered goods to the plaintiff as a carrier on his own account, but on account of the company, and judgment was entered for the plaintiff, for the value of the hogshead of molasses destroyed, less 25%, the value of the molasses saved.[215]

Another example of through traffic in operation is illustrated by a letter written on 3 December 1870, from the Steam Packet Office, Neath, by the agent, J. L. Matthews, replying to a letter from Messrs R. & J. McTurk of Cnewr, Sennybridge. The letterhead has a list of places to which through carriage was provided similar to that on the 1870 poster. It throws a little light on the relationship between steamer and railway managements and customers. In it, Mr. Matthews wrote that he would discuss the subject of the McTurk letter with the Manager of the Neath & Brecon Railway in a few days, and that he was 'prepared to reduce our present rate second class 15/- to first class 10/- on future lots of tobacco water'. (See Illustration 8 on page 69.) Tobacco water was used as an insecticide.

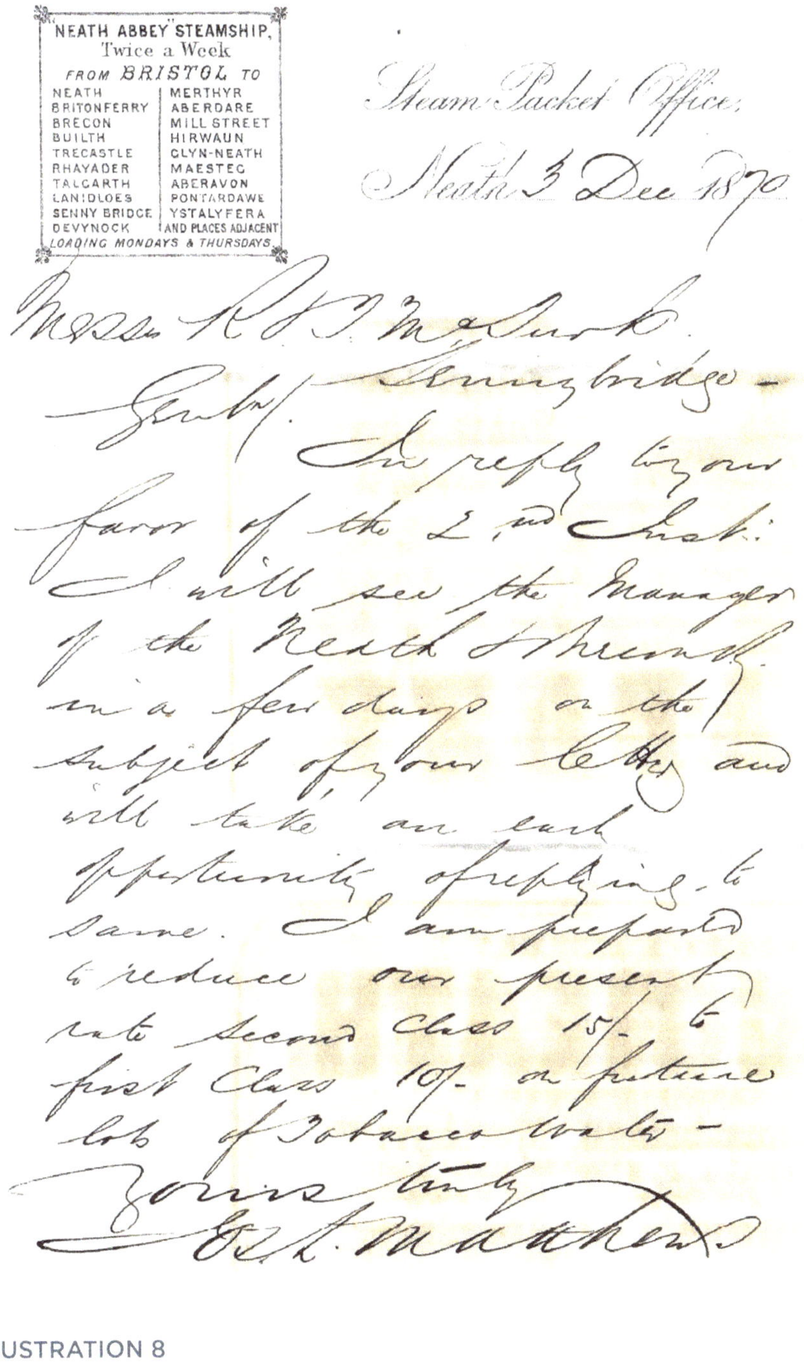

```
NEATH ABBEY STEAMSHIP,
      Twice a Week
  FROM BRISTOL TO
NEATH         | MERTHYR
BRITONFERRY   | ABERDARE
BRECON        | MILL STREET
BUILTH        | HIRWAUN
TRECASTLE     | CLYN-NEATH
RHAYADER      | MAESTEG
TALGARTH      | ABERAVON
LLANIDLOES    | PONTARDAWE
SENNY BRIDGE  | YSTALYFERA
DEVYNOCK      | AND PLACES ADJACENT
LOADING MONDAYS & THURSDAYS
```

Steam Packet Office,
Neath 3 Dec 1870

Messrs R & T McGurk
Gentn/ Sennybridge —

In reply to your favor of the 2nd inst. I will see the Manager of the Neath & Brecon Rly in a few days on the subject of your letter and will take an early opportunity of replying to same. I am prepared to reduce our present rate Second Class 15/- & first Class 10/- on future lots of Tobacco Water —

Yours truly
E. L. Mathews

ILLUSTRATION 8
Letter from the *Neath Abbey* Agent 3 December 1870.

CHAPTER 10

Thefts from Warehouses and the Ship

It was inevitable that cargo traffic attracted the interest of thieves who looked for opportunities to steal from the ship or from a warehouse used for holding goods from or for the *Neath Abbey*. Reports of the goods stolen illustrate the great variety of 'general cargo' or 'sundries' carried by the ship.

The Neath Abbey Steam Navigation Company's warehouse on the Quay at Neath was broken into on 2 April 1847 and a large quantity of groceries was stolen. Four 'excavators,' men working on construction of the South Wales Railway, were arrested and some of the goods were found in their possession. The police were said to be 'in pursuit of their associates'.[216]

At the Glamorganshire Quarter Sessions held at Cowbridge on 5 April William Moore pleaded guilty to the charge of having stolen a cheese, the property of Mr. Evan Evans, Neath. He was sentenced 'to be imprisoned and kept to hard labour for four calendar months'.[217]

When the Glamorgan Quarter Sessions were held at Neath on 29 June Thomas Jones pleaded guilty to the charge of having stolen 100lbs of tobacco, valued at £25, seven whole cheeses, two quarts of wine, 28lbs tea, and various other articles from the storehouse of the Neath Abbey and Bristol Steam Packet Company, the property of Evan Evans and others. He was sentenced to eight months' hard labour.[218]

It is possible that these two prosecution reports relate to different thefts, but the list of goods stolen by Jones probably describes the 'large quantity of groceries' stolen on 2 April.

In 1855 John Minor appeared before the Bristol Magistrates charged with stealing two ingots of copper, the property of the Neath Abbey Steam Packet Company. The ship had arrived at Bristol on the tide on the 14 September and Minor was employed with others to unload her. A custom-house officer apprehended him with the ingots in his possession. He was remanded until

Monday in order to give the company an opportunity of proving the deficiency.[219] There is no further report.

There were reports in December 1862 that for several weeks past there had been a series of robberies from the warehouse of the *Neath Abbey* steamer at Neath. Parcels of goods had been missed from the premises as early as the end of October. More recently goods stolen included two half chests of tea and a large box of boots and shoes. On 10 December, having obtained a search warrant, Superintendent Phillips went:

> to the house of Thomas Quinland, a blacksmith, on the Green, and there, under the roof, through a trap-door in the ceiling, he found fourteen pairs of new boots and shoes, a quantity of twist and other tobacco, a lot of boxes of Lucifer matches, a small bag of tea about 3lbs, a bag of shot and other articles; all of which the Superintendent removed. He afterwards found three false keys, which had been used for admission into the warehouse; they were no doubt of Quinland's own manufacture. He was an excellent workman and a man upon whom previously no suspicion rested.

Quinland was charged along with Annie Hall of Briton Ferry. They were remanded until the following Monday and bail was refused.[220] On 22 December when Quinland and Annie Hall were brought before the magistrate, J. H. Rowland, the court was exceedingly crowded and many waited outside in the hope of getting in. They were charged with a series of robberies from the *Neath Abbey* stores, the property of Evan Evans. After several witnesses had been examined, Hall was discharged, and Quinland was committed for trial at the next Quarter Sessions. Bail was refused.[221]

At the Quarter Sessions, held in Swansea on 16 January, Quinland, aged 33, was 'charged with feloniously breaking and entering a certain warehouse and stealing therefrom a number of pairs of boots and shoes, a quantity of tea, a bag of shot, a quantity of tobacco, and other articles, the property of Evan Evans, at Neath on the 10th December last. The prisoner had made a key for himself and by this means had obtained access to the warehouse and thus carried on a systematic series of plundering'. He was found guilty and sentenced to 'twelve months' imprisonment, the last week solitary confinement'.[222]

Early in March 1867 William Thomas, a Bristol wharfinger, had a quantity of copper ingots brought in by the *Neath Abbey*. On 12 March a wagon load of these ingots was taken from the Welsh Back to the Great Western Railway station, where the driver left it in charge of a boy while he went to fetch another load. The boy saw William Harris, a haulier, walking away with one of the ingots, weighing 14 lbs, and chased him. Harris dropped the ingot and was arrested later. At Bristol Police Court on 28 March he pleaded guilty, and was sentenced to six weeks' imprisonment, with hard labour.[223]

On 11 October 1875, three young men, Andrew Passmore (17), Walter Page (17), and John Evans (18) 'were charged at Neath Police Court with breaking into the Neath Abbey Steam Packet Warehouse at Briton Ferry and stealing nine bottles of sherry wine.' While on duty near the warehouse on Sunday, 10 October, Sergeant Davies of the Neath Police saw a light flash inside. He found the door ajar and went in. Passmore came towards him but dropped the three bottles of wine he was carrying. The Sergeant gave Passmore in charge of Police Constable Hand, went further in and found the other prisoners who had three bottles of wine near each of them. 'The prisoners were employed in works situated close at hand, and were supposed to have committed the act merely for the sake of getting drunk.' They were committed for trial at the Quarter Sessions at Swansea on 18 October at which they pleaded guilty 'to having broken into and entered the warehouse of David Bevan, and stolen therefrom a wooden case and 12 bottles of sherry wine, the property of David Bevan, at Briton Ferry, on the 10th of October, 1875. They were each sentenced to six calendar months' imprisonment'.[224]

CHAPTER 11

Accidents, Other Mishaps and Rescues

The Bristol Channel can be a dangerous shipping route. At over 14m (46ft) its tidal range is the second highest in the world and there are currents of up to 7 knots (8.1 mph). In the nineteenth century the Channel and the River Avon connecting Bristol to it were very busy waterways with a mixture of sailing ships and steamers. Inevitably there were accidents, and the *Neath Abbey* was involved in several, either as one of the parties to a collision in which she or the other ship lost a mast or had the funnel knocked down, or an accident in which she went to the aid of another ship. Occasionally mechanical breakdowns occurred and there was sometimes carelessness. Also accidents happened on board ship.

An early accident involving the *Neath Abbey* occurred on the evening of Tuesday, 5 September 1848, when the *Talbot*, bound for Carmarthen, and the *Neath Abbey*, bound for Neath, collided while sailing down the River Avon from Bristol. The main mast of the *Talbot* was 'knocked nearly overboard,' and the collision 'caused great consternation amongst the passengers, who were, however, speedily assured that no danger was to be apprehended'. After a delay of a couple of hours she continued her voyage. This report also stated that it had 'heard that the fault lies entirely on those in charge of the *Neath Abbey*, who wished to get before the *Talbot*, and in their endeavours to do so caused the collision; their conduct is, therefore, much to be reprehended. We have heard that the *Neath Abbey* was much more severely damaged than the *Talbot*'.[225] I have not found any other mention of damage to the *Neath Abbey*. The *Talbot* was the third iron screw steamer built at Neath Abbey Iron Works. Launched on 14 May 1847, she was bigger than both the *Henry Southan* and the *Neath Abbey*.[226]

On 27 February 1851 the *Neath Abbey* went to the aid of the sloop *Phoenix*, which had got on to the Mussel Rocks, a little west of Sker Point, while bound from Swansea to Bristol with a cargo of copper. She had drifted off and got as far as Dunraven, leaking badly, when she hailed the *Neath Abbey* which was on her way from Neath to Bristol. The *Neath Abbey* took her in tow, lent three men to help with pumping, and got her safely to Bristol. In November the owners of the *Neath Abbey* brought an action in the Admiralty Court to claim salvage compensation. 'The property salved was estimated at £7,050'. On 21 November the owners were awarded £150.[227]

John Williams, master of the *Neath Abbey*, wrote a letter to the Editor of the *Bristol Mercury* in November 1851:

> May I beg your indulgence in inserting the following. On Wednesday, the 19th inst. at 6.15 a.m., the steamer *Neath Abbey*, under my command, was on her passage from Bristol to Neath, and at that time abreast Aberthaw, about one and a half miles from the north shore, when the look-out called, "Port the helm," which was immediately done to avoid a collision with a large steam-ship (afterwards ascertained to be the *Rose*, bound to Bristol from Ireland). It is an established rule, when steamers are meeting, always to port the helm, so that each vessel may pass on the right-hand side; the *Rose*, instead of doing so, put the helm the contrary way, and the consequence was that we very narrowly escaped coming into collision, and experienced some delay. I have to add that, although it was still dark, the *Rose* had not a single light visible. My only reason for troubling you with this is to put other masters of vessels on their guard.[228]

As described in Chapter 5 the *Rose* had been in collision with Evan Evans's schooner *Liverpool Packet* in January 1850, resulting in a successful claim by him against the owners for the cost of repairs and compensation.

During the last weekend of January 1852 while sailing from Bristol to Neath the *Neath Abbey* lost 'the fan of her screw and some other portion of the apparatus. [...] Under the able management of Captain Williams she made the remainder of the voyage under canvas, without further accident, and arrived at Neath on the evening of Sunday, 1 February. She was to have resumed the station on Monday last, but having been taken to repair, it was subsequently determined [...] to give her a thorough overhauling'.[229] The ship was back in service not later than 24 February when she was reported to have arrived at Bristol from Neath.[230]

Under the heading 'Meritorious Conduct of a Captain at Sea' it was reported that on 6 July, 1854:

ACCIDENTS, OTHER MISHAPS AND RESCUES

As the *Neath Abbey*, steam packet, Capt. John Westlake, usually plying between Bristol and Neath, was on her trip from the former place to the latter – the wind blowing a good stiff breeze at the time – when they arrived in view of the Nash sands a vessel, apparently in distress, was perceived, and the Captain immediately made for her, when he discovered it was a Spanish brig, lying at anchor near the sands, and all the crew disabled. The tide was receding fast, which made it more difficult and dangerous to approach her, but after a little delay Capt. Westlake succeeded in placing some of his men on board of her, and took the vessel into Penarth roads. The boatswain had lost several of his toes, and all the crew were more or less injured. They are now under medical care, and it is to be hoped they will soon be convalescent.[231]

Less than 8 weeks later, during the night of Sunday, 27 August, a German ship, the *Lucie* of Oldenburg, bound from Cardiff with coal for Bremen, sank on the Nash sands; the crew got into a boat and were picked up on Monday by the steamer *Neath Abbey* and landed at Cardiff.[232]

A remarkable rescue was reported in August 1868:

On Tuesday last [25 August] one of the most extraordinary and providential escapes perhaps on record occurred under the following peculiar circumstances:–The *Neath Abbey* steamer was, about two o'clock on Tuesday morning, steaming down within two miles north-west of the Holmes [sic]. The night had been intensely dark, and consequent on the late storm the sea was running high. Some lights in the vessel's course caused the captain to slightly alter her bearing, when he fancied he heard a voice, out away on the port bow. The vessel's speed was eased, and on getting within hail a boat was lowered, into which three men at once entered. They made for the direction in which the sound appeared to be, and in so doing lost sight of the vessel's lights, thus increasing the danger of their position. After being nearly an hour in search they discovered a sailor in the water, holding on by a small ladder fastened as a raft to two small pieces of board. On enquiry, he proved to be a native of Picton, Nova Scotia, named Dan Beddie, who had shipped on board a vessel, in which, according to the custom which seems to be so infamously prevalent, he was most harshly treated, and, preferring the chance of a watery grave to the probability of a continuance of the ill-usage, he made the attempt, so happily terminated, to escape from the ship. We need scarcely add that he was taken on board the steamer and most kindly cared for, Captain Evans, with his usual generosity, presenting him with the means of reaching another port whence he could obtain a vessel bound for his native place.[233]

'Captain Evans' was Evan Evans, the owner of the *Neath Abbey*. The master of the ship at this time was almost certainly Daniel Evans who succeeded John Westlake.

On Wednesday, 3 May 1876, while the *Neath Abbey* was going alongside the stage at Briton Ferry to take in freight for Bristol, a fireman, William Leach of Bristol, was killed. 'The engine was being reversed, and deceased, who was subject to fits, was warned by the engineer that he was going to reverse'. When the engineer looked to where he had last seen Leach he saw he was down on the floor. He immediately stopped the engine, and when he got to Leach he 'found his head hurt. It is supposed that he fell forward in a fit, and that the "eccentric" struck him on the head, a portion of hair, &c., being stuck fast to one of the belts connecting the "eccentric" band'. At the inquest held at the police station on the following afternoon a verdict of Accidental Death was returned.[234] According to that report William Leach was married with two children. Another newspaper described the *Neath Abbey* sailing up the river to Bideford on Friday afternoon with her flags flying at half-mast and said that the fireman, whom it did not name, 'was a steady young man, about 30 years of age, and leaves a wife and four children to mourn their loss. Mr. Bevan, the owner of the steamer, generously paid the funeral expenses'.[235] 'Mr. Bevan' was David Bevan, whose wife, Mary, had inherited the ship from her father, Evan Evans, when he died in 1871.

The *Neath Abbey* arrived at Sharpness on Saturday, 20 February 1886 with a cargo of copper from Burry Port. On the 21 February she left empty for Bristol. The master was Isaac Brown. While sailing up the Avon to Bristol she was involved in an incident which led to a claim in the Bristol County Court on 7 May brought by the Corporation of Bristol against the Neath and Bristol Steam Navigation Company, then owners of the *Neath Abbey*, having bought her from Mary Bevan. The claim was 'for damages alleged to have been done to their crane barge by a collision with the steamship *Neath Abbey*, caused by the negligent navigation thereof by the defendants or their servants in the river Avon on the 21st February 1886. The Amount claimed was £5 15s 7d'. The Corporation stated that on 21 February they were having work carried out just below the suspension bridge and they had a barge with a crane on board moored out of the way of the navigation and properly lighted. A steamer coming up the river on the tide ran into this barge causing damage to it. The defendants did not dispute the damage but denied that it was caused by their ship, and the captain of the *Neath Abbey* and three men on board denied that she had been involved in a collision. On the other hand, the captain of the *Bulldog* which had been moored nearby said that he had recognised the *Neath Abbey*. 'He had known her ever since he was a boy. Knew her by her shape. There was no other steamer trading to Bristol of her size which was similar in shape. The next morning he saw the *Neath Abbey*, and a lot of scratches on the plates of her starboard bow, and some of the scroll work near the figurehead was damaged'. The captain of the *Neath Abbey* claimed that had been caused by a collision with a trow in Bathurst Basin, although Mr. Wintle, acting for the defendants, said he would show that she was run into by a barge at Sharpness. The judge gave judgement for the plaintiffs for the amount claimed.[236]

There are other brief reports of minor collisions that attracted little publicity. On 2 January 1878 the *Neath Abbey* had her mainmast smashed and her funnel knocked down when she and the barque *William Paterson* collided below Round Point on the River Avon. The barque was not damaged.[237] On 22 March 1881 the *Neath Abbey* collided with the *Comet* in the River Avon while the latter was arriving at Bristol from Dundalk.[238] The steamer *Iolanthe* arriving at Bristol with general goods from Aberaeron was in collision with the *Neath Abbey* in the River Avon on 19 September 1890, 'sustaining damage to her port bow, rail, covering board, guard rail, &c'.[239]

Accidents happened in port as well as at sea.

Violent gales struck South Wales on Sunday and Monday, 7 and 8 February 1869. On Monday afternoon while the *Neath Abbey* was at Neath a crew member, Edwin Spindlow, an able seaman, aged 36 from Bristol, was drowned.[240] The circumstances of his death were reported in the press:

> while the "Neath Abbey" steamer was lying at her moorings, one of her crew got into a boat to take a rope across the river, when he incautiously stepped on the gunwale while broadside on to the current. The act caused the boat to capsize at once, and the poor fellow was thrown into the stream, which, in consequence of a strong "fresh," was running very swiftly at the time. A rope was thrown to him, and the poor fellow attempted to grasp it: this he unfortunately failed to do, and the current carried him down. The body was not afterwards seen, and up to the present time it has not been recovered. He was a native of Bristol, and was married, but had no family.[241]

Another report stated that the seaman was swept off the boat while 'attempting to take two of his messmates on board'.[242]

David Jones, one of the crew of the *Neath Abbey*, was missed from the vessel while she was lying at Bristol on Monday, 6 May 1872. His body was found in the Floating Harbour on the following Sunday evening. His parents lived at Rosser Street, Neath.[243] He may have been the David Jones, aged 28, born at New Quay, Cardigan, an able seaman who joined the ship at Neath on 22 May 1871.[244]

Henry Light, a married man with no children, was engaged to help unload the *Neath Abbey* at Barnstaple on 10 August 1877. 'A long plank was laid from the quay across the hatchway of the vessel, and the goods were taken out of the hold by a steam winch. [Light] stood in the middle of the plank, which was made of three-inch deals, bolted together' and had to take sacks of maize on his shoulders. Unfortunately, the hook at the end of the winch's chain caught on the plank and tilted it causing him to fall about 16 feet into the hold on to a lot of rod and bar iron, injuring his head badly. He died in the North Devon Infirmary on the following day. At the inquest, the Coroner remarked 'that it was clear from the evidence that no blame could be attached to anyone, and saying he was glad to hear that, while the men were paid well, no allowance was made to them in the way of beer, so that, in the present case, there was no question as to deceased being sober'. The jury returned a verdict of Accidental Death.[245]

It was common practice for 'hobblers' to be engaged to give help to a ship in various ways such as assisting with mooring or giving assistance when a ship was being manoeuvred in harbour or in a river in difficult positions. Hobblers rowed themselves in small boats. On 12 October 1885, David Evans, a labourer of Bull Lane, Carmarthen, married with six children, was drowned while hobbling the *Neath Abbey* in the river Towy. At the inquest held on the following day by Mr. J. Hughes, the Borough Coroner:

> Thomas Davies, mate of the *Neath Abbey*, said that the vessel left Carmarthen Quay at 8.30 for Llanelly, the deceased accompanying in his boat for the purpose of assisting in "slewing" the steamer around the point. At the railway bridge the deceased said he was coming on board directly to beg a pint of beer from the captain. In four or five minutes afterwards witness saw the boat full of water, and Evans holding on to the rope which attached it to the steamer. Witness turned to stop the engine, and when he looked again the boat and Evans had disappeared. The steamer was going at half-speed, and there was nothing in its wash

to swamp the boat. The probability was that in trying to get on board the deceased drove the bow of the boat under water. The steamer was stopped, and they searched for the body for about an hour without success. Later in the day the body of deceased was found about half-a-mile below the railway bridge. The jury returned a verdict of "Accidentally drowned."[246]

CHAPTER 12

Crew

Who were the men who sailed as master or as members of the crew of the *Neath Abbey* and where did they come from?

The main sources of information about crew members are the half-yearly 'Account of Voyages and Crew' that each ship's master was required to prepare and hand in to the appropriate port official. These are also referred to as 'List D.' There is also a little information about masters with the ship's Registration documents. Newspapers' 'shipping intelligence' reports of ships' departures and arrivals frequently named ships' masters. Information has also been gleaned from Censuses and associated Marriages and Deaths records at UK Census Online.

Men signed on a ship at the beginning of each half year even if they had remained on board at the end of the previous half year and were discharged at the end of the six months even when they remained on board. If they joined or left the ship during the period, the appropriate dates were recorded. At the end of every half-year masters of ships engaged in the Home Trade, that is in trade between ports in Great Britain and Ireland, were required to give to the Shipping Master at the ship's home port a signed List D, an 'Account of Voyages and Crew of Home Trade Ship'. The master was required to enter information of every man employed on the ship during the period, including age or year of birth, place of birth, capacity in which employed, and dates of signing on and discharge. There were also Half-yearly Agreements setting out the terms of employment and pay rates which every man had to sign in front of a witness. Allowing for the period the ship was laid up during 1888 and 1889 there were eighty-four half-years for which documents were compiled but documents for only forty have survived, three half-yearly Agreements and thirty-seven Lists D. The earliest is for the first half of 1866.

In 1845 the Board of Trade introduced 'a system of voluntary examinations of competency for men intending to become masters or mates of foreign-going British merchant ships. The system was made compulsory in 1850 and extended to masters and mates of home trade vessels in 1854. A master's or mate's certificate of competency was issued to each man who passed the examination.' There was a transitional period during which men who already had sufficient experience as master or mate could obtain a certificate of competency without examination.[247] The List D form was amended to provide for entry of a man's certificate number, if any. In some cases a bare number was entered, in others the number was preceded by C. C. or C. S. depending on whether it recognised competency or service. In the information that follows I have quoted certificate numbers where they were given. Because masters did not always enter this information and were not consistent in their practice it should not be assumed that the absence of a number necessarily means the man had no certificate.

The three Half-yearly Agreements that have survived are for the periods January to the end of June 1878 and January to end of December 1879. They show that during the first of those periods the master, then James Clibbett, was paid £2 5s. 0d. per week. He did not enter his wages for the other two periods. All three show that the mate was paid £1 10s. 0d., the engineer £2. 0s. 0d., and seamen and firemen were each paid £1 6s. 0d.[248] These three Agreements have entries that show that the crew were required to find their own provisions. I do not know whether this was standard practice or not.

A comparison may be made with the wages of tinplate workers and railwaymen. During a lock-out in the South Wales tinplate industry in 1874 a letter from 'Locked Out' was published in *The Cambrian*. At the time tinplate workers were paid according to their output. The writer declared that rollermen, the most skilled workers in a tinplate mill, received average weekly wages of £2 for 44 hours. Doublers got £1 15s. and furnacemen £1.[249] On the railways, wages varied according to grade. During the 1870s engine drivers earned from 5s. to 7s. 6d. a day and firemen were usually paid about three fifths of the enginemen's rate. Goods guards' pay ranged from £1 1s. to £1 16s. a week, while shunters received between £1 and £1 5s. a week.[250]

The names of approximately 150 men are known. There is some information about all the masters and some of the mates and engineers, but little about other members of the crew.

Masters

In advertisements the master was referred to as 'Commander' for many years. The first man to command the *Neath Abbey* was Thomas George.[251] He continued to sail as master until the end of August 1847 although before that he was occasionally replaced by John Williams. Thomas George became part owner and master of the smack, *Abbess*, owning 32 shares. (The other shares were owned by a Neath grocer, Thomas Winewood, or Winwood.)[252] The *Abbess* was of 42.23 tons and had been built at Neath in 1836 by N. B. Allen. She traded between South Wales ports, mainly Neath, and the West of England, with some voyages to Ireland. Thomas George died on 28 February 1848 at the Vernon Arms, Briton Ferry, after two days' illness. He was only 38 years of age.[253] His shares in the *Abbess* passed to his widow, Sarah George, and she sold them to Edward Boone, who was Agent for the *Neath Abbey* from August 1846 to August 1847.[254]

John Williams became the regular master on 1 September 1847[255] and continued until August 1852. The 1841 census recorded that he was 25 years of age and was living at Neath Abbey with his six brothers and sisters and their parents, John, an engineer, and Elizabeth, both born at Briton Ferry in 1791. In 1851 John Williams, Master Mariner, and his wife, Mary, born at Baglan in 1816, were living at 35 Graig, Briton Ferry, with a son, Thomas, and three daughters, Elizabeth, born in 1847, Mary and Joanna. In 1871 John & Mary Williams, their daughter, Elizabeth, with another son John born in 1853, were living at 14 Railway Terrace, Briton Ferry, on Census night, 2 April.

On 1 June 1871, there was a grand concert at the Assembly Rooms, Briton Ferry, 'for the benefit of Captain John Williams of Alma-terrace, formerly of the *Neath Abbey* steamer, but for many years, bedridden'. The appeal on his behalf was 'heartily responded to'.[256] A second entertainment for his benefit was given on 18 December 1871. Unfortunately, 'there was but a scant attendance owing probably in measure to the wet weather, the programme was a good one, and well carried out, and it is to be regretted that the proceeds after paying expenses will scarce be worth acceptance'. It was said that another entertainment 'for the same deserving object' would be given shortly but a report has not been found.[257]

Perhaps the reference to Alma Terrace is an error or perhaps John and Mary Williams stayed there temporarily in the home of one of their children. On 11 February 1873 Mary 'the beloved wife of Captain John Williams' died at Railway Terrace aged 57.[258] After a long illness Captain John Williams 'quietly died' on 18 May 1880 at 14 Railway Terrace, Briton Ferry, in his 64th year.[259]

John Westlake, born at Watchet in 1804 or 1805, succeeded John Williams as master on 6 August 1852.[260] His master's Certificate was No. C. S. 120,394. Before joining the *Neath Abbey* he had been master of the *Liverpool Packet*, a schooner bought by Evan Evans and John Giles, both brewers at Neath, in November 1847. Evan Evans held 48 shares and Giles 16. In October 1849 Giles sold his shares to Evans. She was a 67-ton schooner, built in 1835 at Bideford and previously registered at Bridgwater.[261] The *Liverpool Packet* traded between Watchet and South Wales ports, chiefly Cardiff. John Westlake had been master of her for at least four years before she was bought by Evans and Giles, and he continued as her master until he replaced John Williams as master of the *Neath Abbey*. He remained master until 21 December 1867, when he left the ship at Bristol.[262] On 31 December 1867, 'Mr John Westlake, Captain of the *Neath Abbey* steamer,' married Mrs Ann Griffiths at St. Thomas's Church, Neath.[263] In 1871 he was described as 'Retired Captain Merchant,' living at 47 Claremont Street, Bristol, with his wife, Ann, born at Neath in 1811, and one daughter and one son from his first marriage. Living with them as a General Domestic Servant was Mary Hopkins, aged 21, born at Neath. He was probably the John Westlake born in 1804 whose death was registered in the Clifton district of Bristol in the second quarter of 1876. In 1881 his widow Ann, aged 67, born at Skewen, Neath, and described as a Ship Captain's Widow, was living with her older sister Jane Beard, a Gardener's Widow aged 76, at 9 The Parade, Neath. The death of Ann Westlake was recorded at Neath in the third quarter of 1890.

On 21 December 1867 Westlake was succeeded as master by Daniel Evans who had previously been master of the *Gratitude* of Swansea and had left her on 19 December at Neath.[264] He continued as master of the *Neath Abbey* until May 1875. His master's Certificate was No. 86,588. The place and year of birth were recorded variously as Briton Ferry 1827 or Fishguard, Pembrokeshire, 1828. However, the 1871 Census gives his age as 42 and his birth place as Goodwick, Pembrokeshire. During his time as master of the *Neath Abbey* he lived at Briton Ferry, at Victoria Place and 10, Albert Terrace, Neath, and then at Neath Abbey. Unfortunately he had domestic problems, as shown by a Notice he issued on 29 March 1870 saying that he would no longer be answerable for any debts contracted by his wife, Eliza Evans.[265] On the night of the 1871 Census, 2 April, the *Neath Abbey* was moored at Bristol and Eliza Evans was on board with her husband. On 1 May 1875 he became master of the *Princess of Wales* owned by the Newport and Bristol Screw Steam Packet Company and sailing between Newport and Bristol.[266] The 1911 Census recorded that Daniel Evans, born in 1828 at Goodwick, Retired Mariner, and his wife, Eliza, born in 1831 at Aberaeron, were living at Arba, New Quay, Cardiganshire. They had been married for 60 years. Both were bilingual. One child had been born alive to them and was still living.

James Clibbett was master of the *Neath Abbey* from May 1875 to 1881. His Certificate was No. C. C. 100,911. He had served as mate of the *Neath Abbey*, from July 1866 to 21 December 1867 having previously sailed on the *Calypso* of Bristol.[267] No record has been found of him from that date until he succeeded Daniel Evans on 1 May 1875. Clibbett was named as master when the commencement of the *Neath Abbey*'s service from Bristol to Ilfracombe and Bideford was advertised on 20 May.[268] He remained in command until 24 March 1881 when Henry Davies signed on.[269] However Clibbett sailed as master a number of times during 1882, especially during the month of June.[270]

The 1851 Census lists James Clibbett born at Northam, Devon, in 1826 and his wife Ann born at Littlehampton, Devon, in 1828, living with their daughter, Mary Anne, born in 1849, at New Street, Northam. Later records list him as born at Appledore which is within the district of Northam. There are records of the deaths at Bideford of Mary Anne Clibbett in 1856 and Anne Clibbett in 1858. In the 1871 Census James Clibbett was living with his second wife Hannah at 1 Crosley Row, Clifton, with three children, the oldest of whom, also named James, was born in 1862. By 1881 they had two sons and two daughters and were living at 11 Wood Crescent, Bristol. His wife had changed her name to Honor. In 1891 they were living at 10 Argyle Place, Clifton, and he was described as a Mariner, so perhaps he had not retired completely. Honor Clibbett died in 1896. By 1901 James Clibbett had become Chief Brother of the Merchants Alms House, King Street, Bristol, originally set up for sick and elderly sailors. He died there on 24 June 1906, aged 80.[271]

Henry Davies, who previously sailed on the *Cambria* of Llanelli, signed on as master of the *Neath Abbey* on 24 March 1881.[272] The Census of 1881 shows that he was on board while she was moored at Briton Ferry on the night of 3 April 1881, and gives his age as 49 and place of birth as Llangrannog, Cardiganshire. Davies continued as master until 1 January 1886 when he was succeeded by Isaac Brown[273] who had relieved Davies on occasion before that, for example on 11 November 1885 when he commanded the *Neath Abbey* on her crossing from Burry Port to Sharpness with copper.[274] Brown was master when, as already described, the *Neath Abbey* was in collision with a crane barge belonging to Bristol Corporation in the Avon on 21 February 1886.[275] Born at Bridgwater in 1840, he held Royal Navy Volunteer's Certificate 65,318. On 10 June 1886, after a short spell on the *Cambria*, Henry Davies took over the *Neath Abbey* temporarily 'in place of Brown whilst at Drill' and continued until 7 August when Brown resumed command. He remained as master until the ship was laid up at Llanelli on 17 November 1887 due to the legal proceedings for winding up the Neath and Bristol Steamship Company, owner of the ship.[276]

The 1881 Census lists Isaac Brown, a Mariner, aged 40, born in 1841 at Bridgwater, living at 85 Philip Street, Bristol, with his wife, Mary, aged 43 and two daughters, Mary and Nellie. Log Books for the period from I July 1886 to 30 June 1887 give his address as 57 Phillip Street, Bedminster, Bristol. In 1911, a widower, he was living with his daughter Mary and her husband, William Boyle, and their step-daughter, two daughters and a son at 3, Albert Road, Staple Hill, Bristol.

Henry Davies, who had preceded Brown, was named as master again from 15 May 1890 while the ship was still laid up. He continued as master until 14 May 1894.[277] William Morgan, who served on the *Neath Abbey* as an able seaman from 30 June to 25 October 1892, and had re-joined the ship on 5 June 1893 as mate, succeeded him as master.[278] Davies was named on some days in early June, but from 14 June until she was wrecked on the night of 19/20 June the master was Morgan. This information from the Crew Lists is not consistent with evidence given by R. H. Gunning at the inquest when he said that Morgan had been master for nearly three months when the ship was wrecked.

William Morgan was born at Swansea in 1858 or 1859. In 1878 he married Elizabeth Olden, or Oldin, also born in Swansea in 1859. The 1881 Census records them as living at 24 Jersey Street, Swansea with Elizabeth's parents, James and Anna Oldin, and her three brothers, one of whom was Thomas William Oldin, aged 10. William Morgan was described as 'Seaman'. In 1891 William and Elizabeth Morgan and their four children were living at 13 Mount Pleasant, Swansea, with seven boarders, three of whom were Elizabeth's father, James Olden, and two of her brothers, but not Thomas. From 5 June to 16 August 1893 Thomas Olden, born in 1870 or 1871 at Swansea, sailed as an able seaman on the *Neath Abbey* while William Morgan was mate.[279] The Morgan children in 1891 were Phoebe born in 1882, Anne born in 1884, William born in 1887 and Mary born in 1888. When *Neath Abbey* was wrecked in June the Morgan family was living at 7, Orchard Street, Swansea.[280]

Mates

Stephen Ings, aged 68, born at Fareham, Certificate No. 41639, was mate during the first six months of 1866. He had sailed on the *Neath Abbey* in 1865 but it is not possible to say whether he had been mate at that time.[281] Ings was succeeded by James Clibbett, who sailed as mate from 1 July 1866 until he was discharged on 21 December 1867.

Clibbett was succeeded by Griffith Evans, born at Neath in 1843, who had joined the ship as a seaman in 1865.[282] He must have taken the necessary examination to obtain a Certificate of Competency because in 1870 he is recorded as having C. C. No. 101,403.[283] He continued as mate until the end of 1879. On 23 February 1880, at Briton Ferry, he signed on the *Titania* as an able seaman, signing off at Briton Ferry on 2 April, signing on again there on 10 April.[284] A strange move, perhaps. The explanation may be that he knew John Rees, a part-owner of the *Titania* who sailed as her mate. *Titania* was a wooden brigantine, 198 tons, built at Prince Edward Island in 1867 and registered at Swansea. Griffith Evans and John Rees, born at Aberporth in 1821, both lived at Briton Ferry. On 7 July 1880, while sailing from St. John's, Newfoundland, to Miramichi, New Brunswick, *Titania* struck an iceberg in fog and sank 50 miles SE of Cape Spear Newfoundland. John Rees was drowned.[285] The rest of the crew including Evans had taken to the boats and were rescued the following morning by the crew of a fishing schooner. They were signed off at St. John's on that day and landed at Liverpool from the steamer *Nova Scotian* on 16 July.[286]

Griffith Evans returned to the *Neath Abbey* as mate on 8 April 1881, having spent some time on another steamer, the *Marne* of Plymouth. He remained on the *Neath Abbey* until 28 June 1883 when the ship was laid up for a new boiler.[287]

In 1881 Griffith Evans, his wife and two children, Ann born at Neath in 1870 and Lewis born at Bristol in 1878, were living at 22 The Warren, Briton Ferry, as visitors in the home of William and Sarah Michael. In different censuses his wife's name is given as Jenner, Jenet and Janet, and her place of birth is confused between Rhymney, Monmouthshire, and Rumney, Cardiff. In 1891 the Evans family were living at 9, The Kennel, Briton Ferry. The 1901 Census lists Griffith Evans, his wife, their son Lewis, their daughter-in-law, also called Janet, born at Llansamlet, and two grandchildren living at 9 Kennel Row, Briton Ferry. Griffith Evans was no longer a mate at sea but was working as a labourer at a local chemical works. In 1911 he was a lighterman at the chemical works, presumably a more skilled job than that of labourer. He and his son, Lewis, both widowers, were living at 10 Kennel Cottages, Briton Ferry. The death of a Griffith Evans, aged 79, born 1843, was recorded at Neath in the first quarter of 1922.

While Griffith Evans was sailing on the *Titania* and the *Marne*, Edwin Thomas, born at Pill, near Bristol, in 1838, was recorded as mate from 1 July to 5 October 1880.[288] David Rees, born in Carmarthen in 1825, succeeded him as mate of the *Neath Abbey* on that date, having previously sailed on the *Cambria* of Llanelli. His Certificate was No. 6,808. The 1881 Census lists him as mate on board the *Neath Abbey* moored at Briton Ferry on Census night, 3 April. He signed off the *Neath Abbey* on 7 April 1881.[289] His wife, Mary, died suddenly on 1 December 1880, when their address was Island House, Carmarthen.[290]

Thomas Davies, born in Cardigan in 1851 or 1852, joined the *Neath Abbey* as a Seaman on 23 April 1881[291] having previously sailed as mate on the *Arbitrator* of Llanelli. In March 1883 he became mate and continued to sail as mate until at least late 1885 when, as described in Chapter 11, a hobbler helping to manoeuvre the *Neath Abbey* in the river below Carmarthen was drowned on 12 October.[292]

As mentioned earlier William Morgan had sailed on the *Neath Abbey* as a seaman in 1892 before becoming mate in 1893.

William Bailey, of St. Thomas's, Swansea, was mate and in command when the *Neath Abbey* struck the rocks at Nash Point on 19 June 1894. He was born at Bristol in 1854, and seems to have joined the ship as a seaman in May 1894, becoming mate when William Morgan became master. He survived the wreck because he and the donkey boy had been ordered to take one of the ship's boats in order to put out a kedge anchor and, unable to return to the ship, they sailed to Barry. In evidence given at the inquest he said that 'he knew her some years. He was on board her some two and a half years ago. He had been aboard this time about five weeks'.[293]

Engineers

The earliest Crew List that has survived is for the first six months of 1866 and only one reference to an engineer on the *Neath Abbey* in earlier years has been found in newspapers. He was John Williams, a married man aged 46, born at Briton Ferry, who was recorded as being on board the *Neath Abbey* on Census night 7 April 1861.

The first engineer recorded in the surviving Crew Lists was William Richards who was engineer during the first six months of 1866 and was listed as having remained on board at the end of 1865. On the List D for the second half of 1870, which is unusual in that the master, Daniel Evans, recorded the dates on which each member of the crew originally joined the *Neath Abbey*, he is recorded as having joined her at Neath in May 1863.[294] He was engineer with Certificate No. C. S. 2744, until he was discharged at Neath on 3 May

1872. At some time after that he served on the *Jubilee* of London but sailed on the *Neath Abbey* again from 1 October 1878 to 1 November 1879. In 1879 his wage was £2 a week.²⁹⁵ He is probably the William Richards listed in the 1841 Census as an engine fitter, born in Cwmfelin, Dyffryn Clydach in 1821 and living there with his father, Thomas, a collier, his mother, Mary, both born there in 1781, and two older brothers. Dyffryn Clydach was the Registration District that included Neath Abbey and Cadoxton, Neath. Cwmfelin is the location of the main buildings of the Neath Abbey Iron Works. He may have been the William Richards, engine fitter, a widower living with his two daughters and one granddaughter at 7 Graig Maesmelyn, Neath, in 1881.

During the first part of the period separating William Richards's two periods of service, the engineer was Thomas Evans, aged 55, born in Llansamlet. He held Certificate No. 2574 and was engineer from 25 May 1872 until a date in 1874, probably 1 July, when the ship was laid up at Bristol.²⁹⁶ He may have been the Thomas Evans, engineer, born in Llansamlet in 1816, who was recorded in the 1851 Census as living with his wife, Elizabeth, also born at Llansamlet in 1816, in Union Road, Neath. David Williams, aged 34, born at Neath, holding Certificate No. 11523, succeeded him on 10 August 1874 just before the *Neath Abbey* returned to service on 19 August. He had previously sailed on the *John Brogden*.²⁹⁷ . He was noted as remaining aboard at the end of 1874 but the Crew Lists for 1875, 1876 and 1877 have not survived.

Robert Nethercott, born at Bristol or possibly Bridgwater in about 1828, who held Certificate No. 11,126, was engineer on the *Neath Abbey* from 23 January until 1 October 1878. He signed on again on 3 November 1879, having served on the *Calypso* of Bristol for a while, and continued until 7 December 1880.²⁹⁸ He may have been related to Henry Nethercott, born at Bridgwater in 1841, who served as an able seaman on the *Neath Abbey* in 1874 and later and is mentioned under 'Other Crew Members.'

John Charles, born at Llanelli in 1836 or 1837, a fitter who had been living on shore, signed on as engineer of the *Neath Abbey* on 7 December 1880. The 1881 Census records John Charles as being on board the *Neath Abbey*, moored at Briton Ferry, on Census night 3 April. He was described as aged 45 and married.²⁹⁹ On 22 January 1883 he was succeeded by William Dunn of Bristol. William Phillips, born at Llanelli in 1856 or 1857, signed on as engineer on 28 November 1883, having previously been working ashore. He signed off on 11 November 1884, when he was succeeded by Nelson Lewis, born 1857 at Bristol, who remained on board at the end of the year.³⁰⁰

Robert Dorman, born in 1848 at Wigan, is listed as engineer during the first half of 1886, having remained on board at the end of 1885. He was noted as remaining on board at the end of June but in the List for the second half of the year is described as born in 1854 at Newcastle-on-Tyne. He was discharged on 2 December 1886.[301] He may be the Robert Dorman, born 1848 at Wigan, recorded in the 1881 Census as living as a lodger in the home of the Rawlins family at 23 Westend [sic] Terrace, Margam. He was described as Engine Driver Tin Mills. The 1891 Census records him as a Stationary Engine Driver living at 92 Morfa Cottages, Margam, with his wife Esther born at Newport, Monmouthshire in 1865 and their daughter Jane E. born in 1886. In the 1901 Census Robert and Esther with their daughter Elizabeth Jane born at Taibach in 1886 and three sons, Harry, Robert and Clifford, all born at Margam Colliery, were recorded as living at 2, Ffrwdwyllt Cottages with two boarders. Robert senior was now a Colliery Engine Fitter. The three addresses are all in Taibach, Port Talbot.

David Davies, born in 1852 at Newquay, succeeded him and remained until the ship stopped sailing on November 17, 1887. He signed on again on 22 July 1890 prior to the ship returning to service on 7 August 1890 and remained until January 1891.[302] He may have been David Davies, seaman, aged 28, born at Newquay, and living there at 24 Park Street in 1881 with his wife, Anne, aged 25, born at Llanarth, and their son, John aged 2.

He was followed by William Baldwin, born in 1855 or 1856 at Bristol, who had sailed on the ship as a fireman in 1880 and 1884.[303] He signed on as engineer 28 January 1891 and remained until 3 January 1894, apart from a few weeks commencing 10 May 1893 when Frederick Baldwin, described as born at Bristol in 1859, served as engineer.[304] (Frederick Baldwin was listed as stoker during the six months beginning 1 July 1893.)[305] The 1871 Census shows that William Baldwin, only 15, was already listed as a mariner. He was the son of Joshua Baldwin, also a mariner, and had four brothers. The oldest was George aged 18, another mariner. Frederick was 11 and Henry was 9, both listed as Scholars. The youngest was James who was two years of age. The family was living at Spring Street, Bedminster, at the time. Frederick succeeded Henry as stoker on the *Neath Abbey* on 25 April while William was Engineer.[306]

Thomas Carlyle, born in 1855 at Truro, Certificate No. 18721, who had previously sailed on the *Antelope*, joined the ship on 2 January 1894 and was discharged on 17 March.[307] Thomas Thomas, born in 1864 at Swansea and holding RNV Cert. No. 8729 [?] joined the ship on 17 March, having previously served on the *Sussex* and was discharged on 4 May 1894. According to one of the three versions of List D for the period January to

19 June 1894 John James, of whom no details are provided, joined the *Neath Abbey* on 7 May and served as engineer but was discharged on 19 May. Two of the three versions name another Swansea man, George Richards, born in 1856, as engineer from 4 May until discharged on 19 May.[308] Thomas Thomas, who was reported to be a married man living at 37 Gerald Street, Swansea, signed on again on 9 June and drowned when the *Neath Abbey* was wrecked on 19 June.[309]

Other Crew Members

George Saunders or Sanders, born at Neath in 1842 or 1843, signed on the *Neath Abbey* as a fireman on 2 January 1867, having previously been working at the Red Jacket Copper Works on the right bank of the River Neath opposite Briton Ferry.[310] He was noted as having remained on board at the end of that year but the Lists for 1868 have not survived. He was on board as a fireman at the beginning of 1869 and remained on board until July 1871. In the 1871 Census he was one of two Firemen on board *Neath Abbey* moored at Bristol on Census night 2 April. He was described as 28 and married. During the second half of 1871 he is recorded as having sailed on the *Frederick Snowdon* of Grimsby until he was discharged at Cardiff on 22 December. He re-joined the *Neath Abbey* on 26 December as cook and was noted as remaining on board[311] but is not on the List for the first half of 1872. Swansea Mariners website states that George Saunders, fireman, born in 1845 at Neath, joined the *Eagle* of Swansea at Neath on 7 February 1878 having previously been on the *Murton*. He signed off at Hayle on 5 April 1878. It lists him as signing on the *Neath Abbey* on 1 October 1878. But the Crew List does not include him. The *Neath Abbey* Crew Lists for 1879 record him as sailing as fireman on her at a wage of £1 6s until he was discharged on 1 November at Bristol.[312] He was almost certainly the George Saunders recorded in the 1851 Census as nine years of age, one of seven children of Joseph and Elizabeth Saunders living at Redjacket, Coedffranc, Neath. In the 1861 Census they were living at Crown Cottage Rows, Coedffranc, and he and his father were copper smelters.

John Maunders (also Manders, or Mouder), aged 44, born at Plymouth, is recorded as a seaman on the *Neath Abbey* during the first half of 1866, having sailed on her in 1865. At the end of June 1866 he remained on board, and sailed on her throughout 1867. The Crew Lists for 1868 have not survived but he is recorded as having been on board throughout 1869, 1870 and the first half of 1871.[313] His association with the ship had begun before 1866. In

January 1863 he was a seaman on the *Neath Abbey* when he was assaulted by John O'Flaherty, another seaman on board. At Bristol Police Court on 10 January O'Flaherty was convicted and fined 10s. and costs, or fourteen days imprisonment.[314]

Thomas Morgan, born in Aberaeron in 1846, signed on the *Neath Abbey* on 4 May 1872 as cook having previously sailed on the *Prince Cadwgan* of Aberystwyth. During 1873 he was on board as a steward. In 1874 he was described as an able seaman on the ship and signed off at an unknown date in 1875.[315] On 1 February 1876, aged 30, he died in Aberaeron at the house of his father, Captain Morgan of the *Farmer's Lass*, having been 'for many years on board' the *Neath Abbey* and the *Princess Alexandra*.[316] Although advertisements for the *Neath Abbey* refer to a Steward or Stewardess on board, Thomas Morgan is the only one identified.

Henry Nethercott, born at Bridgwater in 1841, a member of the Royal Navy Reserve (No. 50,406), signed on the *Neath Abbey* as an able seaman on 10 August 1874 having previously sailed on the *Hannah* of Bridgwater in 1871. He remained on board at the end of 1874 but there is no information of him again until he signed on as an able seaman on 23 January 1878 and remained on her until 18 March 1879. He is not mentioned on the next two Crew Lists but on that for July to December 1880 he is listed as having remained on board from the previous half year and was then signed off at Neath on 23 December 1880.[317] He was possibly the Henry Nethercott listed in the 1851 Census as a Mariner's son, aged 8, living at North Street, Bridgewater. In the 1881 Census, described as a sailor, he was living with his wife, Harriett and eight children at Adelaide Cottage, Chatterton Square, Bristol. Ten years later, now a Labourer, he and Harriett were living at 29 Wesley Terrace, Bedminster, Bristol with four of the children listed in 1881 and three born since then. In 1911 Henry, a Warehouseman, and Harriett were living at 22 Stevens Crescent, Totterdown, Bristol, with their youngest child, Lillian May, now aged 22. Harriett Nethercott died in 1924, aged 79, and Henry J. Nethercott died in 1927 aged 85.

William Baldwin has already been mentioned as an engineer during the period from July 1891 to the beginning of January 1894. However, prior to that he had sailed on the *Neath Abbey* as a fireman, having joined her on 4 February 1880 after sailing on the *Devon*. He was not on the Crew List for the second half of 1880. He returned to the *Neath Abbey* at the beginning of January 1884 and was discharged on the 5 August.[318] He began his service as engineer on 28 January 1891. As already mentioned at least three of his four brothers went to sea. Two of them, Henry born 1870 and Frederick born

1872, sailed on the *Neath Abbey* as stokers. Henry joined the ship on 1 April 1892 and was discharged on 25 April. Frederick replaced him on 26 April and seems to have remained until 3 January 1894.[319]

From 5 June to 16 August 1893 Thomas Olden, born in 1870 or 1871 at Swansea, sailed as an able seaman on the *Neath Abbey*. As explained earlier he was almost certainly the brother-in-law of William Morgan, then sailing as mate.[320]

When the *Neath Abbey* was wrecked James Goody, a married man of East Street, Bedminster, Bristol, an able seaman, and Thomas Llewellyn, a married man from Swansea, a fireman, were both drowned.[321] Richard Richards, aged 18 of Bedminster, Bristol, was the donkey man. After the ship struck the rocks, he went with the mate William Bailey in one of the ship's boats to put out a kedge anchor but could not get back to the ship and sailed to Barry.[322]

Edwin Spindlow and David Jones have already been mentioned in Chapter 11 as having drowned while serving as seamen on the *Neath Abbey*.

CHAPTER 13

Owners

It was recorded in Chapter 3 that the first owners of the *Neath Abbey* were Evan Evans, Jonathan Rees and Paul Evans French. They were co-partners holding the 64 shares jointly. Evan Evans (1794–1871) was born at Ynysmaerdy, Briton Ferry. After some years as landlord of the Grant Arms, High Street, Neath, he became established as a brewer at the High Street Brewery, Neath. In June 1850 he bought the much larger Vale of Neath Brewery at Cadoxton, Neath for £1,520.[323] He and his son-in-law, David Bevan, built up the Evans & Bevan brewing and coal mining businesses, well-known in South Wales for more than 100 years. Paul Evans French, a druggist carrying on business in New Street, Neath, died at Neath on 10 May 1847, 'highly and deservedly respected, aged 28'.[324] Jonathan Rees was a member of a prominent Quaker family in Neath where his father, Evan Rees, had established a business as ironmonger in 1770–1773. He died in 1869.[325]

During 1847 there are references to the owners as the Neath Abbey Steam Navigation Company,[326] the Neath Abbey and Bristol Steam Packet Company[327] and the Neath Abbey Steam Packet Company.[328] These references suggest that the ship was owned within a company structure even if reporters were not sure of its precise name. However, there is no other evidence for such a structure and the use of these names may have been simply a marketing convenience.

The *Neath Abbey* was offered for sale by auction at Bristol on 18 September 1855.[329] I have found no other information about this sale. Perhaps this gave Evan Evans an opportunity to increase his shareholding. Green states that when the ship was re-registered in 1865 Evan Evans owned all the shares.[330] He must have become sole owner well before that year given his occasional private use of the ship from at least 1860, as described in Chapter 8.

The ship was re-registered in 1871 not long before Evan Evans died on 12 April. The Registrar of the Port of Swansea was not informed of his death until 1 April 1886, when his daughter, Mary Bevan, signed a 'Declaration by a Representative of a deceased Owner taking by Transmission' (Form No. 13). In this she informed the Registrar that Evan Evans had died in 1871, that he had not left a Will and that Letters of Administration of his Estate and effects had been granted to her by the Court of Probate on 12 July 1872.[331] It is remarkable that her father, an astute and most successful businessman, did not leave a Will. Masters of the *Neath Abbey*, who must have been aware of his death, continued to enter his name as owner on the six-monthly Crew Lists until July 1880.[332]

In December 1880 it was reported that the Neath and Bristol Steam Tug Company Limited, proposed 'to acquire the screw steamer *Neath Abbey*, and the goodwill of the existing trade of general carrier, carried on by Mr David Bevan between the ports of Neath, Briton Ferry, &c and Bristol. It was registered.10th inst. with a capital of £2,000, in £50 shares'. The report listed seven people as the first subscribers owning 27 shares, among them D. A. W. Baile, New Road, Llanelli, described as an estate agent, two shares, William Thomas, Welsh Back, Bristol, wharfinger, four shares and J. L. Matthews, Water Street, Neath, steam-ship agent, one share.[333] William Thomas may have been the Thomas of Thomas & Co, agents for the *Neath Abbey* at Bristol for most of the time between 1846 and 1887. Matthews had been the agent for the *Neath Abbey* at Neath since 1859 although Baile appears to have become Managing Agent in mid-1880. Before the announcement of this company there must have been negotiations with David Bevan about the possibility of it acquiring the *Neath Abbey* from his wife Mary, who was the owner, and discussions must have continued afterwards. There is no more information about the company, so it does not seem to have been set up. Perhaps there were not enough subscriptions for shares. The ship remained in the ownership of Mary Bevan, the daughter of Evan Evans, until April 1886 when the *Neath Abbey* was sold to the Neath and Bristol Steamship Company.

The proposal to set up the Steam Tug company is relevant to a change in information given on the Crew Lists and Agreements. Until the end of 1879 the six-monthly List D had a box for entering the Name and address of the 'Owner' in the earlier years or, in later years the 'Managing Owner'. Up to the end of June 1880 Evan Evans was named as Owner or Managing Owner even though he had died in April 1871. The printed List D information requirements changed in 1880 and now it was necessary to insert the name and address of the 'Registered Managing Owner or Person appointed under the 38 & 39 Vict. c.88'. This legislation was the Merchant Shipping Act, 1875, Section 4 of which declared:

The term "managing owner" in sub-section one shall include every person so registered as managing owner or as having the management of the ship for and on behalf of the owner.

The point of this change seems to have been to make clear the name of the person who had a legal responsibility to ensure that when a ship put to sea she was in a seaworthy state. (The Act is best known for requiring a line to be painted on the side of the hull to show the maximum depth to which the ship could be loaded safely, the Plimsoll line.)

On List D for the second half of 1880 this person was named as 'D. W. Bell, Llanelly, Carmarthen'.[334] D. W. Bell is an error for D. A. W. Baile of New Road, Llanelli, who is named on all the half-yearly reports available for the remainder of the period when the ship was registered at Swansea, with one exception. That was the List D for the first six months of 1882 when the information given was 'Neath and Bristol Steamship Co. Neath'.[335] However, the ship's owner was still Mary Bevan. The latest half-yearly report available before the ship's transfer to the Bristol Registry in 1886 is that for July to December 1884.

It is not possible to determine why the sale of the ship did not take place before 1886. Perhaps David Bevan was not satisfied with the price the would-be purchasers were prepared to pay, perhaps Mary Bevan, whose legal rights of ownership as a married woman had been strengthened by the Married Women's Property Act of 1882, was not prepared to sell. However, this is speculation. In April 1886 events moved swiftly.

On 3 April 1886 Mary Bevan wrote to the Registrar of the Port of Swansea requesting him to transfer the Registry of the *Neath Abbey* to the Port of Llanelli.[336] An index card in the Ships Register for Llanelli at the Carmarthenshire Archives shows that the ship was registered at Llanelli on 6 April with the Port No. 1/1886; that she was acquired from Mary Bevan by the Neath and Bristol Steamship Company Limited by Bill of Sale dated 15 April and that she was transferred to the Bristol Registry on 16 April 1886.[337]

In the Bristol Register of Ships the owner was described as 'The Neath and Bristol Steamship Company Limited, having its principal place of business at Llanelly in the County of Carmarthen,' owning all 64 shares. 'David Archard Williams Baile of Caerithin [*sic*], Llanelly in the County of Carmarthen' was designated as the person to whom the management of the vessel was entrusted by and on behalf of the owners. Baile was the steamship company's secretary. The company took out a mortgage for £700 plus interest at 5% per annum dated 24 April 1886, registered 29 April. The Joint Mortgagees were

Arthur Baker, Francis Frederick Fox, both of Bristol, David Evans, Corn Merchant, and David Archard Williams Baile, secretary of the steamship company, both of Llanelli.[338]

In 1887 a petition was brought in the Liverpool District Registry by D. A. W. Baile for the winding up of the company on the ground of insolvency.[339] An order for winding up was made in January 1888.[340]

During late 1889 there appears to have been a dispute between Baker and Evans and Baile over a proposal to sell the ship. This resulted in a case in the Chancery Division on 21 January 1890 before Mr Justice Kekewich. Evans and Baile, the defendants, did not appear in court and the case seems to have been dropped.[341]

The *Neath Abbey* was sold at auction to an unnamed buyer for £325 in April 1890.[342] By Bill of Sale sale dated 27 November 1890, the Joint Mortgagees sold her to Arthur Baker and Francis Frederick Fox as Joint Owners. They in turn sold the ship to Robert Harding Gunning of Broad Quay, Swansea, on 8 May 1891. On that date Gunning took out a Mortgage for £1,250 plus interest at 6% per annum. The Joint Mortgagees were Arthur Baker and Francis Frederick Fox. Gunning appointed himself Managing Owner on 29 July 1891.[343] In bankruptcy proceedings during August 1894 he said he had purchased the ship for £1,270.[344] One wonders how he could have thought it sensible to pay that sum, financed by mortgage, for a ship that had been auctioned a little more than a year earlier for £325. He remained owner until the ship was wrecked in June 1894.

Thus the history of the ownership of the *Neath Abbey* began with one of the three joint owners when she was launched in 1846 on his way to becoming an outstandingly successful business man with significant interests in the brewing and coal industries and ended with a man who, through a combination of poor judgment and bad luck, had a dismal end to his business career.

CHAPTER 14

Agents

The owner of every ship needed an Agent as his representative in each port used by that ship. The Agent's responsibilities included liaising with the port authority or harbourmaster in respect of entering, berthing and leaving; paying dues; ensuring availability of labour to load or unload the vessel; warehousing goods accumulating in advance of the loading day and goods unloaded from the ship if not taken away that day; making the necessary arrangements for delivery or onward carriage if goods were not to be collected from the wharf by the consignee; arranging for the provision of any supplies, including coal, required for the vessel; and arranging for any necessary repairs. Some owners used their own staff located at a port to carry out these responsibilities but for a ship like the *Neath Abbey* locally situated agents were more likely to be used.

Advertisements show that when the *Neath Abbey* started sailing in August 1846, the agents were Thomas & Son, Back, at Bristol, and Edward Boone at Neath.

Over the years there were many changes. In June 1849 C. W. Smith, Welsh Back, replaced Thomas & Son at Bristol. In June 1850 the Agent was named as Smith & Trickey but in October William Trickey was agent and continued until the end of 1851. William Morgan was Agent from 1 January 1852 until Thomas & Son, Welsh Back, regained the Agency in June 1852. Thomas & Son continued as Agent for the *Neath Abbey* until December 1887 when the ship had stopped sailing because of a winding up petition brought against the owners, the Neath and Bristol Steamship Company.[345] When the ship resumed sailing in August 1890 they were named as agents again but only during August and September. From 6 October 1890 until the ship was wrecked, Stone and Co were the Bristol agents.[346]

Advertisements show that A. H. Buckett succeeded Edward Boone as Agent at Neath in August 1847 and continued until December 1849. From January 1850 John Jones, Neath, became the Agent there. Later his address was given as 'Quay, Neath,' and he continued as Agent until at least 5 June 1852. On 11 July 1852 the Agent at Neath was Wm. Morgan Jones, Quay, Neath, but by 9 October 1852 James Williams had become the Neath Agent. He continued to act as Agent until at least the end of July 1857 when he issued a Notice that the *Neath Abbey* was 'now removed from her Station between Bristol and Neath' for 'some important and immediate repairs'.[347] The next reference found for the Neath Agent is on 29 June 1859, when he was named as Joseph L. Matthews who continued to be named as agent until 1880. The last reference I have found to him as Agent for the *Neath Abbey* is in *Slater's Directory for North & South Wales 1880*:

> CONVEYANCE BY WATER.
> TO BRISTOL (calling at Briton Ferry and Port Talbot), the *Neath Abbey Steamer*, from the Quay, Monday, Thursday & Friday, according to tide – Joseph L. Matthews, agent.[348]

As has already been mentioned, D. A. W. Baile of Llanelli was the managing agent from mid-1880. Nevertheless, frequent reports of sailings during 1884 with general cargo name Matthews as agent.[349] I assume that, unless he was acting on behalf of Baile, he was not acting as agent for the ship after mid-1880 but simply as a shipping agent who had booked cargo space on her.

R. H. Gunning was agent from February to November 1887, when the *Neath Abbey* stopped sailing because of the winding up petition. No agent was needed at Neath when *Neath Abbey* began sailing again in August 1890 because she sailed from Swansea to Bristol, not from Neath. Gunning of Broad Quay, Swansea, acted as agent for the owners. When he bought the ship in May 1891 and set up the regular Swansea to Bristol service at the beginning of August Gunning did not need to employ an agent.[350]

More information about Matthews and Gunning is given in the Appendices.

CHAPTER 15

Offices, Wharves and Warehouses

In August 1846, when the *Neath Abbey* commenced the Neath to Bristol service, she used the Town Quay located immediately downstream of the Neath River Bridge.

At first advertisements gave the address of the agent simply as 'Neath,' but from 1852 the address in the advertisements of the ship's monthly schedule was 'Quay, Neath'. In advertisements for through carriage of merchandise in 1868 and 1869 the address was 'Packet Office, Neath'. The letter from the agent J. L. Matthews to J. & L. McTurk 3 December 1870, already referred to, is written on paper with the printed heading 'Steam Packet Office, Neath'.

There were warehousing facilities available for goods carried by the *Neath Abbey* from the start of her service. Advertisements from 1 August 1846 included a Notice that 'Goods consigned to order, or not taken away before Six o'clock in the evening of the day of landing, will be warehoused at the risk and expense of consignees'.[351] That the *Neath Abbey* had dedicated warehouse premises, not a shared facility, is demonstrated by the report referred to in Chapter 10 of a robbery at 'the Neath Abbey Steam Navigation Company's warehouse on the Quay at Neath' on 2 April 1847.[352]

By July 1851 the ship was using the Neath Abbey Wharf.[353] In the December 1862 report of the prosecution of Thomas Quinland for theft of goods from the warehouse of the *Neath Abbey* steamer the agent, J. L. Matthews, gave evidence that 'the drawer in my office' on the wharf had been broken open.[354] That may have been an office devoted to the business of the Warehouse only with the rest of the business to do with the ship being carried on at an office on the Quay. The address of the Agent was given as 'Quay, Neath' as late as 2 September 1871.[355]

This wharf was described variously as the 'Neath Abbey Wharf', the 'Steam Packet Wharf', or the 'Neath Abbey Packet Wharf', and was located a little way downstream of the Town Quay backing on to the continuation of the Green, the road that separated the riverside buildings from the Neath Canal and thus well-placed for transhipment of goods sent down the Neath Valley by canal. (The Neath Abbey Wharf should not be confused with the wharves at Neath Abbey on the right bank of the river. They were used by the copper works and the collieries located in the vicinity of Neath Abbey.)

In 1872 *Mr. Brereton's Report with Plan on the Floating of the River Neath* was published.[356] The 'Floating of the River' was the scheme described in Chapter 4 for the construction of a straight navigable channel up to Neath avoiding the severe bend in the river, and the conversion of part of the bypassed channel into a floating harbour. It has a plan of the river from the town of Neath to its mouth. Part of this plan showing the riverside buildings for a short distance downstream from Neath River Bridge is included as Illustration 9 on page 101. The Town Quay, named Corporation Wharf, on this plan and the Steam Packet Wharf are clearly marked.

Maps identify the premises immediately upstream of the Neath Abbey Wharf as Allen's Quay[357] or the Dinas Brickworks[358] which in 1845 was owned by the firm of Young and Allen.[359] Allen was Nicholas Bowen Allen and he was also the Allen of Allen and Luly [*sic*], wooden shipbuilders of Neath, whose premises were probably either on the brickworks site or next to it. Allen held his property as a tenant of the Gnoll Estate and may have subleased part of it for the establishment of the Neath Abbey Wharf. As already mentioned, in 1840 Allen and Luly built a wooden steam tug at Neath called the *Dragon Fly*. She was fitted with her single 32in grasshopper side lever engine at the Neath Abbey Iron Works[360] and was the first steam-propelled vessel built at Neath. When she was launched in 1840 the 64 shares were owned jointly by Nathaniel Tregelles of the Iron Works, John Rowlands, a banker, and Evan Thomas, a gentleman. In 1852 following the death of Evan Thomas, sale of the shares resulted in 23 shareholders. Among them were Nathaniel Tregelles two shares, John Rowland twelve, Joseph Tregelles Price four, Jonathan Rees two, Nicholas Bowen Allen one, and also one share held by Thomas Clement, 'Artisan', who was one of the men credited with building the *Neath Abbey*.[361] On 24 June 1847 Nathaniel Tregelles of Neath Abbey married Frances Allen, daughter of John Allen of Liskeard in the Friends Meeting House at Liskeard.[362] The 1851 Census shows that Nicholas Bowen Allen and James Luly were both born at Mevagissey in Cornwall. So there were links between the Tregelles, Price and Allen families in terms of family, county of origin and business in Neath. Were the Allens of Liskeard related to the Allens of Mevagissey? It may be

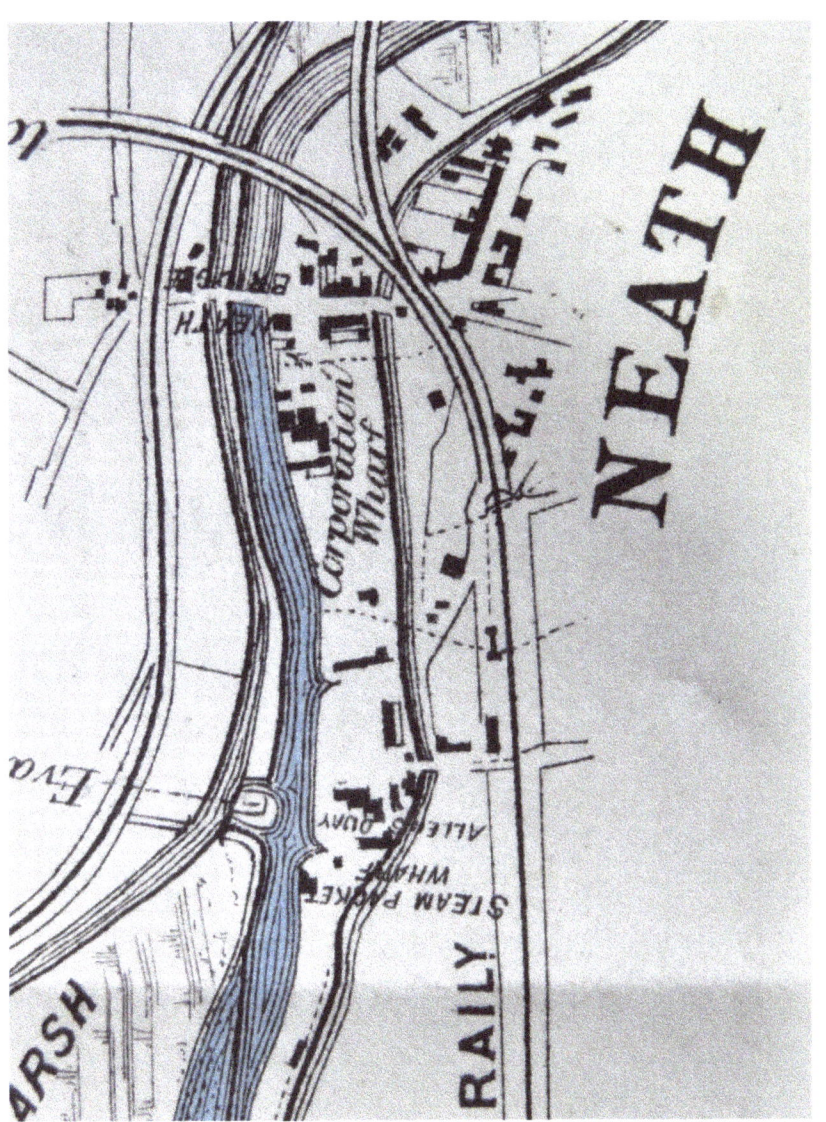

ILLUSTRATION 9
The Neath River from the Town Bridge to the Steam Packet Wharf, Neath.

of interest that Nicholas Bowen Allen was the great-grandfather of Allen Lane Williams, better known as Sir Allen Lane, the founder of Penguin Books.[363]

The first reference to this wharf that I have found is a report of an accident that occurred on 23 July 1851. A 'person in the employ of John Thomas, who keeps the collecting and delivery vans for goods for the South Wales Railway, at Neath, was conveying a quantity of copper in cakes from the station to the Neath Abbey Packet Wharf; in descending a hill alongside the Neath Canal, the reins became entangled in the shaft, and the horse's head being turned from the right direction, he was driven by the weight into the canal with such force that he was killed on the spot. It was a serious loss to the owner of the horse, as the horse was worth upwards of £20'.[364] The reference to 'a hill' is a little puzzling, but perhaps the short incline from the roadway to the level of the canal bank is meant.

In 1860, Jesse Webber was charged at Neath Police Court with being drunk and disorderly on the Neath Abbey Wharf on 5 September.[365] On 5 January 1862, the body of William Williams was found lying in the river 'off the Neath Abbey wharf'. John Parker, who had spotted the body, 'called the attention of Captain Westlake (who was on board the steamer) to it, and that gentleman procured a boat hook, by which the corpse of Williams was lifted out'.[366]

A series of 'Notes of a Rambler', written by an anonymous contributor, was published in the *Swansea and Glamorgan Herald* in 1867. On 6 April he described walking from the Melin Tinplate Works, past the Chemical Works and on to Neath. 'Crossing the Canal, near to the "Neath Abbey" Wharf, belonging to Captain Evan Evans, whose vessel trades and carries passengers to Bristol and back two or three times a week, I proceeded by the side of the Canal, and I looked with astonishment at the great improvement apparently made in the timber trade of Neath'.[367]

In 1872 it was reported that a Bill to be introduced in Parliament in the next session, in respect of the Neath Harbour Improvement Works, included a clause describing a proposal to build an 'Approach Road, in the parish of Neath, commencing from and out of the public road leading to the Steam Packet Wharf on the River Neath, at or near the bridge over the Neath Canal on the Green in the town of Neath'.[368]

It is assumed that there was a warehouse at the Neath Abbey Wharf when the ship began using it.

In December 1862 Thomas Quinland, a blacksmith, of Neath, and Annie Hall of Briton Ferry were 'charged with a series of robberies from the Neath

Abbey stores, the property of Evan Evans, Esq.' In his evidence, Superintendent Phillips referred to the premise as 'the stores of the Neath Abbey Wharf, the property of Mr. Evans'.[369]

Although the *Neath Abbey* was no longer sailing from Neath, this wharf at Neath was still known as the 'Neath Abbey Wharf' in 1892 when Hopkin Lewis, living at the Green, Neath, was charged with assaulting a policeman while in the execution of his duty. In evidence Constable Cross stated that he was on duty at the Green on Sunday, 28 July. 'At 10.45 he visited the yard adjoining Allen's brickworks, known as the Neath Abbey Wharf' and saw several men come out of 'the old warehouse,' one of whom had a large jar. The constable wanted to see what was in the jar and followed the man, Hopkin Lewis, but Lewis assaulted him, grabbing him by the throat and threatening him. Lewis was fined 40 shillings with costs, or in default one month's imprisonment with hard labour. He was allowed a fortnight to pay the money.[370]

Briton Ferry Dock was opened on 22 August 1861 and in anticipation of this it was advertised that 'On and after the 1st April, 1861, Goods for Briton-ferry [*sic*] will be Discharged into a Warehouse solely for that purpose near the Ferry'.[371] A plan published c. 1860 shows the location of the Steam Packet Wharf on the east bank of the river just upstream from the Ferry and its relationship to Briton Ferry Dock.[372] See Illustration 10 on page 104.

The prosecution of three men for stealing nine bottles of sherry from the Neath Abbey Steam Packet Warehouse at Briton Ferry in October 1875 has already been mentioned in Chapter 10.

Throughout her working life the *Neath Abbey* sailed to and from Bathurst Basin in central Bristol some six miles up the Avon from the Bristol Channel. This was not an easy river to navigate as has been shown to some extent by the mishaps involving the ship. Warehouse facilities were arranged by the ship's agent.

ILLUSTRATION 10
Map of River Neath showing location of Steam Packet Wharf at Briton Ferry.

CHAPTER 16

Disaster

Before giving an account of the events of the night of 19/20 June 1894 a brief description of the coast at Nash Point, Glamorgan, is appropriate. The Point is on a part of the South Wales coast to the west of Barry where the gently undulating land of the Vale of Glamorgan terminates quite suddenly at severe cliffs. Below the cliffs the shore is rocky with extensive rock platforms extending into the sea. The rocks and the Nash Sands, a long sandbank quite close offshore on which many ships have been wrecked, present a significant hazard to shipping. To help mariners avoid these dangers there are two lighthouses on the cliff top, one taller than the other. They were built in 1832. The taller one, 122 ft high, remains in use.[373] It was the practice for coasters to keep close to the shore, sailing through the channel between it and the Sands 'to avoid the current of the tide, which was greater outside than inside'.[374]

The normal crew number at this time was seven. During the second half of 1893 only 8 men sailed on the *Neath Abbey*, one seaman being replaced by another during August. However, in the period between the beginning of 1894 and 20 June there was unusual turnover of crew. Seventeen men are listed on the third and last version of the Crew List. William Morgan, formerly mate, replaced Henry Davies as master in May and Clifford Harley, who had joined the ship during that period as a seaman, became mate. In June he was replaced by William Bailey, who had also joined the ship during that period as a seaman. Thomas Carlyle was engineer at the beginning of the year but was replaced by Thomas Thomas in March. He in turn was replaced by George Richards briefly during May and Thomas Thomas returned as engineer. Other men were Alf. Phillips, Richard Bevan, E[dmund] Bevan and J. Goody, all seamen; Thomas Leafranc and T. Llewellyn, both firemen; Richard Richards (donkey man); and Albert Parker, John James and Henry Stanton whose occupations were not stated.[375]

On 12 June 1894 the *Neath Abbey* was towed back into Swansea with machinery out of order.[376] Nevertheless, after repairs, she arrived at Bristol on

15 June.[377] She left Bristol on Saturday, 16 June with a cargo of general goods and arrived at the North Dock, Swansea, on Sunday morning.[378] On Monday she was discharged.

The *Neath Abbey* left Swansea on the evening of Tuesday, 19 June, with a cargo of flour and tin. She was due to arrive at Bristol at eight o'clock on Wednesday morning.[379] On board were the crew of seven and four passengers. The crew comprised the Captain, William Morgan, of 7, Orchard Street, Swansea, the mate, William Bailey of St. Thomas's, Swansea, the engineer, Thomas Thomas, of 37, Gerald Street, Swansea, the second engineer, Thomas Llewellyn, of Swansea, the donkey boy, Richard Richards, of Bedminster, Bristol, James Goody, seaman, of East Street, Bedminster, and Edmund Bevan, seaman, of 47, Strand, Swansea. Apart from Richards and Bevan all were reported to be married men. The passengers were Frederick Donovan, Shaddick, Tudball and Winter. They were described as 'destitute firemen' who had arrived at Swansea from the United States and wished to get to Bristol.[380] The Crew List records Thomas Llewellyn as a fireman.[381]

During the night *Neath Abbey* was wrecked off Nash Point.

Sunk Off the Nash.

STEAMSHIP GOES DOWN WITH LOSS OF LIFE.

Captain and Three Hands Drowned

VESSEL SEEN ON THE ROCKS.

ILLUSTRATION 11
South Wales Echo 20 June 1894.

The first reports of the tragedy appeared in newspapers on 20 June but have little information other than that the ship had been wrecked and that the captain and three members of the crew had been drowned. Illustration 11 shows the column heading of the report in the *South Wales Echo* on that day. The short report gave the following information:

Our Swansea reporter wires this morning:– A telegram has just been received at Swansea from the Nash Point announcing that the *ss. Neath Abbey* had sunk, and that Captain Morgan and three hands are drowned. The remaining three got ashore at the Nash. How the casualty occurred is not known, and particulars are anxiously awaited. Most of the crew belonged to Swansea. The *Neath Abbey* left Swansea for Bristol last night.[382]

In fact, 'the remaining three' had not got ashore at the Nash. This was one of many errors of fact in the early newspaper reports of the tragedy.

There were reports on 21 June that the ship went on to the rocks during a fog or heavy mist. The *St. James's Gazette* reported that she went on to the rocks during a fog.[383] The *Bristol Mercury* stated that the weather was very misty, and rain fell very heavily.[384] The *Western Daily Press* reported that the 'weather was so rough at the time, and so thick and hazy that, with a drizzling rain, the lighthouse could not be seen'.[385] *Lloyd's List* reported that she 'went ashore on Wednesday morning off the Nash, in a dense fog'.[386] These reports are reflected by Coflein, the online database for the National Monuments Record of Wales which, quoting the *Bristol Mercury*, states that 'the vessel was caught in thick mist and rain, and was grounded on rocks near Nash point'.[387]

Captain Everett of the steamer *Merthyr* which arrived at Swansea on the morning of the 20th is reported to have said that:

when passing the Nash at 4.30 this morning he saw the *Neath Abbey* on the rocks, so close to the land that anyone could walk ashore. There were men on board, and they blew the whistle as he passed. He also saw two men near, pulling in a boat, apparently in search of a tug. They stopped rowing as the *Merthyr* came along, but they did not hail him. The boat evidently belonged to the *Neath Abbey*, which had only one boat left on her davits. As the boat did not hail him, and as the *Neath Abbey* was so close to the shore, he did not go to the vessel, concluding his assistance was not wanted.[388]

However, information given by those involved in the tragedy supports neither the claims about fog or thick mist nor the details of Captain Everett's account.

In a report published later in *Lloyd's List* the mate, William Bailey, said 'Proceeded all well until 9.30 p.m., when we passed the Tuskar [*sic*] Rock seeing also the Porthcawl and Nash Lights steaming about 6½ knots'. He referred to the 'Nash Lights on the port bow' at 11 p.m.[389] At the inquest Edmund Bevan, a seaman, said 'the weather was fine, and all went well until the vessel came up abreast the Nash Lights about 11.45. The weather was still fine, but dark, and occasionally misty'. Also in evidence at the inquest Bailey referred to 'the haziness of the weather'.[390]

At the inquest Richard Wilson the chief officer of the Nash lighthouse said he had been there 13 years and was well acquainted with the sea coast. 'He said that the evidence about the weather was incorrect, the Stareweather and Bull lights being visible. He was called up at midnight. He got up, and saw the lights of the *Neath Abbey* quite visible'. Bull Point Lighthouse is on the North Devon coast, near Mortehoe and about 10 miles north-west of Barnstaple. Stareweather is an error for, or corruption of Scarweather, dangerous sandbanks off Porthcawl.

Richard Wilson also wrote a letter that was published in the *Western Mail* and other newspapers on 28 June.

> TO THE, EDITOR OF THE "WESTERN MAIL."
> Sir, – I wish to correct a statement which appeared in your issue last week concerning the wreck of the steamer *Neath Abbey*. It is stated by your correspondent that the vessel went ashore in thick weather, which is quite a mistake. The vessel went ashore at 11.45; the weather was remarkably clear, all lights visible; also the opposite coast. The fog came on at 3.30, after the unfortunate vessel broke her chains and drifted ashore. – I am, &c.,
> RICHARD WILSON, Principal keeper,
> Nash Light-head.[391]

It is clear from the statements by the mate William Bailey, Henry Stabb light-keeper, Principal keeper Richard Wilson, Eldad Jay the Llantwit coastguard officer, and the seaman Edmund Bevan that the ship struck the rocks close to midnight, that a telephone call from the lighthouse informed the coastguard at Llantwit soon after, that the boat in which Bailey and the donkey boy put out the kedge sailed away to Barry at about 1.30 a.m., and that the ship began to break up at some time up after 2 a.m. None of the survivors mentioned seeing another ship passing.

From evidence given by Bailey, Bevan, Donovan and others at the inquest reported in the *Glamorgan Gazette* 29 June, and reports in the *Cambrian* 29 June, and *Lloyd's List* 2, July (Bailey), *Western Daily Press*, 22 June (Donovan), *Cardiff Times*, 23 June ('a correspondent'), and *Bristol Mercury*, 21 June

(Richards) I have attempted to piece together a coherent account of the unfolding of the tragedy. There is some inconsistency about the time when the ship began to break up, but this is not surprising given the nature of the men's experiences.

The *Neath Abbey* left Swansea at 7.15 p.m. on Tuesday and proceeded up Channel inside the Nash Sands. There was a drizzling rain off Porthcawl. Bailey, the mate, was in charge, the captain being below, but he came on deck occasionally. Bevan, a seaman, was on lookout duty. Everything went well until 9.30 when they passed the Tusker Rock, with the Porthcawl and Nash Lights visible. They were steaming at about 6½ knots. Weather began to get hazy. Their course was S.E.¼E., position half a mile off the coast. At 11 p.m., tide being three-quarter ebb, weather heavy, wind S.W., light with a smooth sea, the vessel was going full speed, Nash Lights on the port bow, steering S.S.E. They kept middling close to land in their usual course, about half a mile off the shore. Bevan was looking out for the buoy on the Nash.

The vessel was proceeding, when she suddenly struck, about 11.30 pm., to the west of the Nash, about a quarter of a mile from the lighthouse and remained. They kept the engines going. She then lifted and they turned her round to her proper course, but the swell drove her in, and she again struck. The captain ran on deck before she struck the second time. The mate told him their position. The captain put the helm hard to port but she stuck fast. Bevan said that when the captain came on deck he ran to the wheel and said, 'Good God, where have you got her?' and put the wheel hard down. The ship began to roll heavily, and the captain then ordered all hands to put the boat out in order to put out a kedge. This was done by the mate and the donkey boy, Richards. When they tried to return to the ship the water had ebbed so much that they could not reach the vessel. They held on to the kedge warp, and when the painter parted at 1.30 a.m. on the 20th they sailed the boat outside the breakers and made for Barry, where they arrived at 7.30 a.m. Before leaving they could not communicate with those on board because of the heavy surf. Heavy seas were washing over her.

The rolling of the steamer resulted in her hull being holed, and when the tide made she began to fill. Those on board could not come ashore, so they tried to launch the other boat, which was smashed. She was then carried round and round by the sea and began to break up. The life-buoys were in the forecastle, and they could not get at them, although they did think of them.

Donovan, a passenger, was in his bunk when the ship struck. After the mate and the donkey boy had gone the captain tried to bring the ship's head round with another ketch anchor but failed in the attempt, and then he asked for assistance from the shore, which was about seventy yards away. The ship was about a quarter of a mile away from the lighthouse. The captain signalled to the lighthouse for the life-saving apparatus, but messages had to be sent to Porthcawl and Llantwit for rocket apparatus. Early on Wednesday Eldad Jay, petty officer of the coastguard, stationed at Llantwit, received a telephone message from the lighthouse that a vessel was ashore at Marcross Cwm. He went there to see how matters stood and then went back to get the life-saving apparatus.

The ship struck at a quarter to twelve o'clock. Winter and Shaddick swam ashore but Tudball, another Bristol man, and Donovan stopped aboard to help the captain. It was hoped that it would be possible to float the ship off at high water. After they had been on board about two hours and a half subsequent to the accident the ship began breaking up, and then those aboard were ordered to look out for themselves.

Bevan went over the side of the vessel with a ladder, but the sea being so rough he had to return. Donovan then stripped and sprang overboard, taking the ladder with him. After a desperate struggle and a hard swim he reached land, and was pulled ashore by Winter and the lighthouse-keeper, in an exhausted condition. About half an hour after he left the ship broke in two, and the six men who were left aboard were thrown into the rough sea, but just then the life-saving apparatus from Llantwit was brought. The men ashore saw Tudball struggling in the water with a life-belt attached to his body. Two attempts were made with the rockets to send a line to him, but he missed them both. However, he swam nearer the shore, and a line being thrown to him, he was pulled in. Another man was seen struggling near Tudball, but he sank before a line could be sent to him.

A sailor, a Bristol man, was seen by Bevan jumping over the side to try and get to the shore. He drowned alongside the ship. The foremast was down. The captain was forward on the bowsprit, from which he either dived into the sea or was cast in, and the second engineer [Thomas Llewellyn, fireman] was washed overboard. The first engineer and Bevan were left on the bowsprit; they were washed off three times and washed back. Another sea came and again washed them off. The steamer had broken in two before this. When Bevan came to the surface, he could not see the engineer. He made for the shore, and finding a plank got hold of it; in the breakers he lost it but found it. This happened several times, until he became unconscious, and he knew no more until he found himself in the lighthouse. They told him he had been picked up by the Llantwit rocket apparatus men about 8.30 a.m. It was daylight when the vessel began to break up – between five and six o'clock.

Bevan could swim but the second engineer and one of the seamen said they could not.

The captain, who was an excellent swimmer, swam within 30 yards of the shore, and one of the rocket apparatus crew, Alfred Chatterton, bravely attempted to go to his assistance, but the heavy ground-sea prevented him reaching the captain, who was carried against the Point and dashed to pieces within ten yards of the rescue party, his cries for help being pitiful to hear.

William Henry Stabb, a lightkeeper at the Nash west lighthouse, was on watch about 11.45 on the night in question in the lantern and distinctly heard the rumbling and the thud of the propellers. He went outside on the balcony and saw the lights. He thought she was very close to the shore. She must have been coming up by the lights facing him. The tide was falling, it was nearly low water. He waited a bit, and heard the engines stop and saw lights moving about the vessel. When he found that he reported the occurrence to the principal lightkeeper. He went out to the cliff, and when he came back said the vessel was ashore. The news was then telephoned to the coastguard at Llantwit. Stabb and one of the keepers from the high lighthouse went down to the seamen and asked them if they were alright. They replied 'Yes'; that they had run an anchor out and had done all they could at present. They said they did not want assistance. During the next 20 minutes two passengers jumped over the side and came ashore. The coastguard from Llantwit, Mr. Jay, arrived and then left to get the rocket apparatus. Stabb and the other lightkeeper remained on the beach. When the coastguard returned, he fired a line across the vessel. The last man was just afterwards washed overboard by the sea. One man came ashore on a ladder, and another was assisted ashore by Alfred Chatterton. They carried two men up to the lighthouse. Dr. Simpson, of Llantwit, descended the cliff-ladder, and restored Tudball to consciousness, and under his care the whole of the rescued men were said to be doing well.

Robert Harding Gunning said he had been the owner of the ship for about three years. Everything on board was in good condition. She was practically rebuilt in 1881. She was insured for £500, being one third of her value. Captain Morgan had been captain for nearly three months, and was, before that, mate of her. He was a steady, sober, and reliable man, and was well acquainted with the coast.

Walter Charles Lewis, a lighthouse-keeper, corroborated Stabb's evidence. He believed the captain thought the vessel would go off and he did too, at one time. At about 3.30 on Wednesday morning, he was on watch and saw the body of the second engineer [Thomas Llewellyn, fireman]. He informed the coastguard, and the body was recovered.

The body of the captain was found by Ebenezer John, a carpenter from Llantwit, about 50 yards off the point at Marcross Cwm. The chief engineer's body was found by David Morgan, a farm labourer from St. Donat's, near Marcross Cwm at about twelve o'clock and at about the same time William Williams of Broughton found the body of James Goody at the same place.

The bodies were taken to Marcross and placed in Holy Trinity Church pending the inquest, which was held at the Horseshoe Inn, Marcross, on 22 June by Mr. Thomas Stockwood, coroner for the Ogmore Division. After hearing the evidence, the jury returned a verdict of 'Accidentally drowned, owing to the *Neath Abbey* keeping in too close to the shore'.[392]

After the inquest the bodies of the captain, Thomas Thomas and Thomas Llewellyn were taken to Swansea for burial.[393]

On 29 June a letter to the editor from Rev. A. A. Mathews, Holy Trinity Vicarage, Swansea, was published in *The Cambrian* appealing:

> 'to all those who are charitably disposed, to help me start in business Mrs. Morgan, the widow of the late Capt. Morgan, who, with three others, were either drowned or killed off the Nash Point last week, in connection with the wreck of the *Neath Abbey*. He might easily have preserved his own life; but first his eagerness to save the ship, and secondly his noble effort to preserve the life of the engineer, brought about his death. He was a good swimmer, and pluckily made for the engineer to try and save him, and had got back within an arm's length of those on shore, when a breakwash came and dashed him against the rocks, which caused his instant death. He has left a widow, a poor delicate woman, with four children, the eldest of whom is a little girl of 11 years of age, utterly destitute. I shall therefore feel very grateful to receive subscriptions towards this most deserving and needy case [...]'.[394]

A week later *The Cambrian* published another letter from the Rev. Mathews acknowledging 12 donations amounting to £8 11s 6d and expressing the hope that he would be able to acknowledge more the following week.[395] I have not found such an acknowledgement or any other information about this appeal which was completely overshadowed by the major fundraising efforts being made at the time for the dependants of the 290 men and boys killed in the explosion at the Albion Colliery, Cilfynydd, on 23 June, three days after the *Neath Abbey* was wrecked.

On 28 June it was advertised that Messrs. Tregerthen Dunn & Co. would auction the wreck of the screw steamer *Neath Abbey* and the anchors, chains, ropes etc. salved from her at 12 noon on 2 July and that the sale would take place 'alongside the wreck near the Nash Lighthouse'.[396]

Reports in *Lloyd's List* show that the total proceeds of the auction of the wreck and of salvage of cargo amounted to £55 13s 8d.[397]

CHAPTER 17

Conclusion

So ended the life of a ship built almost exactly 48 years earlier at the Neath Abbey Iron Works. She had spent nearly all that time within the Bristol Channel. In 1846 when the *Neath Abbey* was launched the great majority of ships trading on the Channel were wooden sailing ships, and the relatively few that were not were small paddle steamers mostly built of wood. Built of iron with screw propulsion in June 1846 she was an example of pioneering marine engineering as there was still scepticism about the suitability of screw propulsion for ocean-going ships. Her career spanned a period during which the nature of merchant shipping changed dramatically as steamships replaced sailing ships to an increasing extent and screw propulsion became the standard. Also during her life communication within South Wales and between South Wales and England was revolutionised by the development of a substantial railway network.

From 1846 to 1887 she sailed regularly between Neath and Bristol as well as sailing to and between other ports on the Channel. During her last few years she continued to sail to Bristol, but from Swansea. Due to the quality of her construction and the skills and hard work of the men who sailed her she played an important role in the Bristol Channel coasting trade throughout her 48 years and made a significant contribution to the commercial life of Neath and the surrounding area. She was well-known and easily recognised in most ports on both sides of the channel.

The Port of Neath is now a shadow of the port known to the men of the *Neath Abbey* but it continues to operate under the control of the Neath Port Authority. Its legal limits and responsibilities still extend to a little above the town bridge in Neath but the effect of the building of a swing bridge across the river by the Rhondda and Swansea Bay Railway Company in 1896 at a point downstream of the confluence of the Clydach and Neath Rivers and its permanent closure in favour of railway traffic in 1986 have resulted in the operational limits now extending only from the south of that bridge to the seaward of the Navigational Channel in Swansea Bay. Briton Ferry Dock closed in 1959 but there remain a few wharves on the riverside at Giant's Grave, and also on the right bank of the river, below the railway bridge, are the Neath Abbey Wharves, originally built to handle coal traffic. These wharves provide berths for ships of up to 6,000 tons. The Port handled 262,817 tonnes of mixed cargo moved by 182 vessels in 2009 but after 2017 the number of vessels fell considerably and in 2022 only 31 vessels carrying 71, 876 tonnes used the Port.[398]

The story of the *Neath Abbey* may be said to be representative of that of the many coasting traders criss-crossing the Bristol Channel day after day throughout the nineteenth century.

In the twenty-first century it is difficult for us to imagine how important shipping services across the Bristol Channel were to the life and the trade of communities on both sides of the channel in the nineteenth century. The ships have gone, most of the harbours they used have become silted up or have been adapted as marinas, and the wharves and warehouses have crumbled away or been converted for other purposes. The men who spent their working lives on the ships have long since passed away and, generation by generation, memory of them has faded. Shipping activity in South Wales is concentrated now on the large ports of Newport, Cardiff, Port Talbot, Swansea and to some extent Barry. Railway transport is far less important than road transport for carriage of goods. Road haulage vehicles of many types travelling on much improved roads provide fast door to door carriage of goods traffic with reduced need for transhipment between railway and road. Car ownership and electronic communications have transformed business and private travel. Not only is it difficult to imagine how important the Bristol Channel coasting steamers were, it is not an exaggeration to say that we have forgotten they existed.

I hope this account helps to promote an understanding of how it used to be.

APPENDIX 1

Is the steamer in the painting by C Hill the *Neath Abbey*?

The painting is believed to date from c. 1848. When the *Neath Abbey* started sailing on 1 August 1846 there were sixteen steamers sailing on routes across the Bristol Channel but only three of them were screw steamers, the *Clara* sailing between Gloucester and Newport, the *Henry Southan* sailing between Gloucester and Swansea, and the *Neath Abbey*. From 1847 to 1852 three more screw steamers appeared on cross-channel routes: the *Princess Royal*, built at Neath Abbey in 1850, sailing between Bristol and Swansea from the autumn of that year, the *Jenny Jones* built at Bristol in 1851, sailing between Bristol and Cardiff and the *Glendower* sailing between Bristol and Liverpool via Swansea.[399] Thus, although the *Neath Abbey* was the only screw steamer scheduled to sail to Neath, there were four others that might have called there either as a diversion from the normal route or on an excursion, the *Clara* and *Henry Southan* from 1846, the *Princess Royal* from 1850 and the *Jenny Jones* from 1851. The *Glendower* at 467 tons can be ruled out.

It seems reasonable to conclude that if the painting dates from between 1846 and 1850 there is a very high probability indeed that the screw steamer shown is the *Neath Abbey*, sailing from Neath on a twice weekly schedule, with the *Henry Southan* being far less likely and the *Clara* even less so. If the painting dates from 1851 or 1852 the *Princess Royal* and the *Jenny Jones* are perhaps remote possibilities. I am inclined to believe that she is the *Neath Abbey*. However, whether she is or not the painting may be regarded as a good representation of a ship very much like her.

APPENDIX 2

Joseph Lloyd Matthews (1834–1897)
Agent at Neath for the *Neath Abbey* 1859 to 1880

Joseph Lloyd Matthews was born at Mynyddislwyn, Monmouthshire, in 1834. His father John Matthews was also born there, and his mother, Sarah, was from Risca, Monmouthshire. Both were born in 1810. In about 1847 John Matthews became the Minister of Zoar Welsh Independent Chapel, Neath, and in 1851 the family were living at East Terrace, Neath. J. L. Matthews was the oldest child and had four sisters. The Census described him as a Brewer's Clerk. The brewer is not identified but may have been Evan Evans with whom he became closely acquainted.

In the fourth quarter of 1859 J. L. Matthews married Catherine Evans, born in Briton Ferry in 1828 or 1831. Possibly the Catherine Matthews who died at Neath in the fourth quarter of 1908. In 1861 J. L. Matthews and his wife Catherine were living at Water Street, Neath, with a servant, Hannah Jones from Glyn Neath. By 1871 they had two daughters and a son, John Henry, as well as a servant, Rachel Thomas from Llansamlet. By 1881 a third daughter had been born and they were living at 7, Arthur Court, Water Street, Neath, apparently without a servant. Their daughter, Mary Evelyn, married Rees Powell Morgan, a solicitor, on 31 July 1883.[400] In 1891 Joseph Matthews and Catherine were still living at 7, Arthur Court with their son and two daughters. He was described as a Shipowner and the son, John Henry, was described as a Shipping Agent. However, in 1901 John Henry Matthews was described as a Wharfinger and in 1911 as a Hay Merchant's Clerk.

Joseph Matthews became the Agent for the *Neath Abbey* at Neath not later than June 1859 when he was 25 years of age.[401] He continued in that role until 1880 when D. A. W. Baile became Managing Agent. Nevertheless, there are frequent reports of sailings during 1884 with general cargo in which Matthews is named as agent.[402] It is assumed that on those occasions he was acting simply as a shipping agent who had booked cargo space on her. He probably continued to act as a shipping agent for some time. Butcher's Directory for 1881 lists 'Matthews Jsph. L. shipping agent, the Quay'.[403]

His father, Rev. John Matthews, was minister of Zoar Welsh Independent

Chapel for 33 years. On 2 April 1868 there was a presentation of a testimonial and address to John Matthews to mark completion of 21 years as minister of the chapel. Evan Evans, the owner of the *Neath Abbey*, who was treasurer of the chapel, presented the testimonial and gave the address. Joseph Lloyd Matthews was secretary of the chapel and conductor of the substantial programme of music.[404]

Joseph Matthews was active in the musical life of Neath. He was choirmaster at Zoar for many years. After his father's death in 1880 he and his family attended the English Congregational Church at Gnoll Road, Neath, where he was choirmaster for 15 years.[405] He was vice-president of the Neath Harmonic Society when it was established in 1868.[406] M. Jules Allard was appointed its first choirmaster but Matthews often conducted in place of him and he succeeded M. Allard as the Society's conductor in March 1878.[407] In 1872 J. L. Matthews led the Neath contingent of the South Wales Choral Union and prepared it for combining with contingents from other South Wales towns to enter the competition for massed choirs at the Crystal Palace in July 1872. The Choral Union won the Challenge Cup and won it again the following year.[408]

In March 1870 J. L. Matthews was elected as one of the two Auditors for the Corporation of Neath and retained this position until at least 1893/4.[409] In March 1893 it was reported that his remuneration was increased from 4 guineas to five guineas. He was also one of the two Auditors of the Neath and District Tramways Company Limited for a period that included 1883.[410]

In December 1880 the Neath and Bristol Steam Tug Company was set up with the purpose of acquiring 'the screw steamer *Neath Abbey* and the goodwill of the existing trade of general carrier carried on by Mr. David Bevan between the ports of Neath, Briton Ferry, &c., and Bristol'. The company was registered with a capital of £2,000 in £50 shares. J. L. Matthews, Water Street, Neath, was listed among the first subscribers with one share.[411] The scheme came to nothing, and the ship remained in the ownership of Mary Bevan, David Bevan's wife, until 1886.

The small steamer *City of York*, 79 tons, built by J. McIntyre at Paisley in 1878, was bought by Matthews in April 1887.[412] There are numerous reports of her cross-channel sailings between Neath/Briton Ferry and Bristol, often with calls at Swansea or Port Talbot.

Joseph Matthews died on 4 January 1897, aged 63, leaving a widow, one son and two daughters.[413] The funeral took place at Llantwit Churchyard, Neath, on Thursday, 7 January.[414]

APPENDIX 3

A Note about R. H. Gunning

Bankruptcy proceedings against R. H. Gunning followed quickly after the loss of the *Neath Abbey*. At the time of purchase in May 1891 he had mortgaged the vessel for £1,250 with annual interest at 6%. Because of her age he had not been able to insure her for more than £500.[415] When she was wrecked, he had paid off by instalments £700 of the £1,270 purchase price of the ship.

At his first public hearing in the Swansea Bankruptcy Court the statement of affairs showed liabilities expected to rank £786 12s. 9d., assets £153 6s 11d., and a deficiency of £633 5s. 10d. The causes alleged were 'the sinking of the *Neath Abbey* steamship, loss of 100 £1 shares in the Hibernian Steamship Line, death of two valuable horses, and the loss of shares in the steamship *King Ja Ja*'.[416]

He was declared bankrupt but on 28 March 1895 he was granted a discharge, suspended for three months, as from 1 April 1895.[417] In March 1898 his stepson, William H. Bevan, married Miss Katie Rees of Swansea. A brief report stated that the couple would go to South Africa where Bevan would take up a 'lucrative position' under his father who was managing a shipping company there.[418]

Endnotes

All Census information quoted in the text has been obtained from *ukcensusonline.com* and I have not thought it necessary to insert endnotes for that information as the Census origin is clear from the text. If I have obtained any information about a birth, a marriage or a death from any source other than *ukcensusonline.com* I have quoted that source in an endnote.

Note on Currency

1. www.officialdata.org.uk/inflation/1850?

Chapter 1

2. Glanmor Williams, 'Neath Abbey' in E. Jenkins (ed.), *Neath and District A Symposium* (Published by Elis Jenkins, Neath, 1974).
3. Harold Carter, 'Growth of Neath Town' in E. Jenkins (ed.), *op cit.*
4. Robert Thomas, 'Communications' in E. Jenkins (ed.), *op cit.*
5. Information from the Neath Port Authority in 2023.
6. For this section I have drawn on Laurence Ince *Neath Abbey and the Industrial Revolution* (Tempus Publishing, 2001), Chapter 5.
7. Keith Tucker, *A Scratch in Glamorganshire* (Historical Projects, 1998), 163.
8. D. Rhys Phillips, *The History of the Vale of Neath* (Published by the Author, Swansea, 1925), 336.
9. Ince, 40.

Chapter 2

10. Ince, 57.
11. *Cambrian*, 21 December 1816.
12. Grahame Farr, *West Country Passenger Steamers* (Stephenson & Sons, 1967), 4.
13. Patrick N. Wyse Jackson in *Dictionary of Irish Biography: www.dib.ie/biography/nimmo-alexander-a6214.*
14. *www.engineering-timelines.com/who/Price_HH/priceHenryHabberley.asp.*
15. Ince, 57.
16. Ince, 58.

17 *Cambrian*, 19 April 1823.
18 Ince, 38.
19 Ince, 58.
20 National Library of Wales. Welsh Tithe Maps. Map of Cadoxton juxta Neath in the County of Glamorgan. Field No. 123 Field Name: Cheadle Works with the Foundry and Furnaces.
21 *Cambrian*, 5 March 1842.
22 Ince, 166; *Cambrian*, 7 May 1842.
23 *Ibid*, 8 October 1842.
24 Ince, 166.
25 *Welshman*, 25 July 1845.
26 Stephen R. Fox, *Transatlantic: Samuel Cunard, Isambard Brunel, and the great Atlantic Steamships* (Harper Collins, New York, 2003), 144.
27 Fox, 147.
28 J. Grantham, *Iron as a Material for Shipbuilding* (Simpkin, London 1842), 5. Quoted by Ince, 59.
29 Fox, 146.
30 *Ibid*, 149.
31 "To the American Public, …" *Scientific American*, vol. 1, no. 1, 1845. JSTOR, http://www.jstor.org/stable/24922002. Accessed 16 May 2023.
32 *Shipping & Mercantile Gazette*, 5 December 1853.

Chapter 3

33 *Welshman*, 12 June 1846.
34 *Cambrian*, 19 June 1846.
35 *Ibid*, 2 August 1845.
36 *Swansea and Glamorgan Herald*, 10 May 1848.
37 *Ibid*, 2 February 1848.
38 Ince, 165.
39 *Monmouthshire Merlin*, 26 October 1850.
40 Green, 107.
41 WGAS   D/D PRO/SR/S/1846/1-7.
42 *Welshman*, 14 May 1847, also *Cambrian*.
43 D. Rhys Phillips, 445–446.
44 Green, 102.
45 artuk.org/discover/artworks/the-river-neath-with-the-ship-viola-154309
46 *The Mechanics' Magazine, Museum, Register, Journal, and Gazette*, Volume 49, Robinson and Co., London, 1848, 211 (Downloaded from https://books.google.co.uk/books/) Also *Cardiff and Merthyr Guardian*, 19 August 1848.

47 *Report of the Twenty-first Meeting of the British Association for the Advancement of Science,* July 1851.(John Murray, London, 1852), 116–117
48 WGAS D/D PRO/SR/S/1846/1-7. (Builder's Certificate and Surveyor's Certificate,13 July 1846.)
49 *Ibid.* (Letter 1 June, 1855, Registrar, Bristol to Registrar, Swansea.)
50 WGAS D/D PRO/SR/S/1865/19.
51 *Swansea and Glamorgan Herald,* 14 October 1865.
52 WGAS D/D PRO/SR/S/1871. (Declaration of Ownership.)
53 *Ibid.* (Letter from Tonnage Dept.)
54 *Ibid.* (Certificate of Survey, 10 Aug. 1874))
55 *Ibid.* (Surveyor's Report on Crew Space, 9 Dec. 1870)
56 Bristol Archives 37908/1/12 (Neath Abbey).
57 *Ilfracombe Chronicle,* 2 October 1875.
58 WGAS D/D PRO/SR/S/1871.

CHAPTER 4

59 *Sailing Directions for the Bristol Channel,* Captain E. J. Bedford, R.N. Hydrographic Office of the Admiralty (1879). Downloaded from Internet Archive 11 May 2023.
60 *Sailing Directions for the Bristol Channel.* By H. M. Denham Hydrographic Department of the Admiralty, (London. 1839), 87–88. Downloaded from Google Books.
61 *Sailing Directions for the Bristol Channel.* 1869. Quoted in letter from 'A Merchant' in *Shipping & Mercantile Gazette,* 30 December 1869.
62 *Shipping & Mercantile Gazette,* 30 December 1869.
63 *Swansea and Glamorgan Herald,* 19 June 1861.
64 *Western Mail,* 27 December 1882.
65 Paul Richards, *Neath Floating Dock,* www.neathantiquariansociety.co.uk/index.asp?pageid=723540

CHAPTER 5

66 *Cardiff and Merthyr Guardian,* 1 August 1846.
67 G. A. Taylor, *Transactions of the Neath Antiquarian Society,* 1937/1939, quoted in Cliff Morgan, *Briton Ferry Notes,* Briton Ferry Y.M.C.A., (n. d.), 5.
68 *Bristol Mercury,* 1 July 1848.
69 *Ibid,* 5 September 1848.
70 *South Wales Daily News,* 15 July 1882.
71 *Swansea and Glamorgan Herald,* 1 March 1848.
72 *Bristol Mercury,* 2 December 1848.
73 *Bristol Times,* 3 January 1852.

Endnotes

74 *Bristol Mercury*, 10 January 1852.
75 *www.swanseamariners.org.uk/shipsregister.php*
76 *Ibid*.
77 *Bristol Mercury*, 31 July 1852.
78 *Cardiff and Merthyr Guardian*, 24 August 1850.
79 *Shipping & Mercantile Gazette*, 3 May 1853.
80 For example, *Bristol Mercury* 20 May, 1 July, 29 July 1865.
81 *Swansea and Glamorgan Herald*, 14 October 1865.
82 WGAS   D/D PRO/CA/S, Neath Abbey, 3948 (1872).
83 WGAS   D/D PRO/CA/S, Neath Abbey, 3948 (1874).
84 *Western Daily Press*, 29 June 1883.
85 WGAS   D/D PRO/CA/S, Neath Abbey, 3948 (1883).
86 *Western Daily Press*, 3 & 11 August; *Cambria Daily Leader*, 10 November 1883.
87 WGAS   D/D PRO/CA/S, Neath Abbey, 3948 (1878).
88 WGAS   D/D PRO/CA/S, Neath Abbey, 3948 (1884).
89 *Swansea and Glamorgan Herald*, 10 April 1861.
90 *Cardiff Times*, 30 August 1861.
91 Farr, 108.
92 *North Devon Journal*, 27 May 1875.
93 *Ibid*, 3 June 1875.
94 *North Devon Advertiser*, 4 June 1875.
95 *Ilfracombe Chronicle*, 9 October 1875.
96 *Ibid*, 2 & 9 October 1875.
97 *Ibid*, 3 July 1875.
98 *Shipping and Mercantile Gazette*, 19 March 1877.
99 *North Devon Journal*, 22 March 1877.
100 *Whittington's Neath Tide Table for the Year 1876* (Whittington, Neath), 50. (*Neath Antiquarian Society Library*.)
101 *Ilfracombe Chronicle*, 6 & 13 January 1877.
102 NAS Aq-6-4-1
103 WGAS   D/D PRO/CA/S, Neath Abbey, 3948 (1878).
104 *North Devon Journal*, 14 February 1878.
105 *Welshman*, 17 December 1880.
106 Farr, 133–4.
107 *Welshman*, 20 September 1872.
108 *Ibid*, 4 April 1873.
109 *South Wales Daily News*, 17 June 1882 & *Bristol Times and Mirror*, 15 January 1883.
110 *Shipping & Mercantile Gazette*, 1 March 1881.
111 *South Wales Daily News*, 1881.
112 *Ibid*, 15 Nov. 1887; *Lloyd's List*, 16 & 18 Nov. 1887; *Bristol Mercury*, 10 March 1890.

[113] Bristol Archives   30182–538 (Neath Abbey).
[114] *Bristol Mercury*, 10 March 1890.
[115] *Lloyd's List*, 19 December 1887.
[116] *South Wales Daily News*, 19 & 28 January 1888.
[117] *Ibid*, 18 April 1890.
[118] *Ibid*, 29 April 1890.
[119] Bristol Archives   37908/1/12 (Neath Abbey)
[120] *Swansea and Glamorgan Herald*, 6 August 1890.
[121] *South Wales Daily News*, 9 August 1890.
[122] *Cambria Daily Leader*, 16 & 21 August 1890.
[123] Bristol Archives   30182/538 (Neath Abbey).
[124] *Ibid*.
[125] *Lloyd's List*, 22 & 27 July 1893.
[126] Bristol Archives   30182–538 (Neath Abbey).
[127] *Lloyd's List*, 27 January 1894.
[128] *Ibid*, 13 February 1894.

Chapter 6

[129] Trevor Boyns and Colin Baber, 'The Supply of Labour 1750–1914,' in *The Glamorgan County History*, Vol. V, *Industrial Glamorgan*, Chapter VII, (Glamorgan County History Trust, 1980), 322–323.
[130] *Report of the Commissioner appointed to inquire into [...] the state of the population in the Mining Districts, 1846* (HMSO, London, 1846). Extract in *The Cardiff and Merthyr Guardian* 5 September 1846.
[131] *Monmouthshire Beacon*, 25 July, 1846.
[132] *Report of the Commissioner appointed to inquire into [...] the state of the population in the Mining Districts, 1846*. Quoted in Richard C. Allen, 'An Indefatigable Philanthropist: Joseph Tregelles Price (1784–1854) of Neath, Wales.' (*Quaker Studies*, Vol 23/2 (2018).
[133] *Welshman*, 10 April 1846.
[134] *Cambrian*, 8 May 1846.
[135] *Ibid*, 2 January 1846
[136] *Monmouthshire Merlin*, 6 November 1847.
[137] *Cambrian*, 11 December 1846.
[138] *Bristol Mercury*, 3 October 1846.
[139] *Ibid*, 16 January 1847.
[140] *Ibid*, 3 June 1848.
[141] *Ibid*, 10 August 1850
[142] *Ibid*, 2 April 1853 & 30 June 1860.
[143] *Aberdare Times*, 2 September 1871.
[144] *Cardiff and Merthyr Guardian*, 4 & 11 September 1847.

145 Information in December 1870 poster. Author's collection.
146 *Western Mail*, 13 September 1871.

Chapter 7

147 Farr, 207.
148 *Cambrian*, 17 April and 12 June 1824.
149 *Cardiff and Merthyr Guardian*, 15 June & *Cambrian*, 22 June 1833.
150 *Welshman*, 14 June 1844.
151 *Cambrian*, 3 August 1844.
152 *Cardiff & Merthyr Guardian*, 4 July 1846.
153 *Ibid*, 1 August 1846.
154 *Cardiff & Merthyr Guardian*, 9 August 1845.
155 *North Devon Journal*, 2 September 1852.
156 *Western Mail*, 9 November, & *North Devon Journal*, 17 November 1870.
157 *North Devon Journal*, 20 July 1848.
158 *Ibid*, 17 June 1852.
159 *Ibid*, 2 September 1852.
160 Martin Phillips, *The Copper Industry in the Port Talbot District*, Phillips, (1935), 63–64.
161 *North Devon Journal*, 14 July 1853.
162 *Ibid*, 19 July 1855.
163 *Welshman*, 20 July 1855.
164 *North Devon Journal*, 2 August 1855.
165 *Bristol Mercury* & *Cardiff and Merthyr Guardian*, 17 May 1856.
166 *North Devon Journal*, 26 June 1856.
167 *Ibid*, 21 August 1856.
168 *Welshman*, 17 June, & *Cardiff and Merthyr Guardian*, 18 June 1859.
169 *Cardiff and Merthyr Guardian*, 25 June 1859.
170 *Western Daily Press*, 10 August 1859.
171 *Cardiff and Merthyr Guardian*, 2 July 1859.
172 *Pembrokeshire Herald and General Advertiser*, 15 August 1862.
173 *Bristol Mercury*, 22 August & *Cardiff Times*, 23 October 1863.
174 *North Devon Journal*, 23 July 1863.
175 *Ibid*, 19 May, & 28 July 1864.
176 *Ibid*, 25 August 1864.
177 *Swansea and Glamorgan Herald*, 20 June 1866.
178 *Brecon County Times*, 27 July & 10 August 1867.
179 *Cambrian*, 7 July 1871.
180 *Ilfracombe Chronicle*, 12 June 1875.
181 *North Devon Journal*, 29 July 1875.
182 *Ibid*, 5 August 1875.

183   *Ibid*, 12 & 26 August 1875.
184   *Western Times*, 20 August; *North Devon Journal*, 26 August & 2 September 1875. The *North Devon Herald*, 1875, was not available online.
185   *North Devon Journal*, 29 June 1876.
186   *Ibid*, 19 July 1877.
187   *North Devon Herald*, 2 August 1877.
188   *Ibid*, 2 & 9 August 1877.
189   Farr, 76.
190   Farr, 227.

Chapter 8

191   John Morris, *op. cit.*, 58.
192   *Shepton Mallet Journal*, 13 June 1862.
193   *Swansea and Glamorgan Herald*, 18 June 1862.
194   *Bristol Daily Post*, 18 June 1862.
195   *Brecon County Times*, 3 August 1867.
196   *Swansea and Glamorgan Herald*, 21 November 1860.
197   *Ibid*, 5, 12 & 19 September 1860.
198   *Western Morning News*, 15 September 1860.
199   *Shipping and Mercantile Gazette*, 17 July & 29 July 1867.
200   *Swansea and Glamorgan Herald*, 7 August 1867.

Chapter 9

201   *Bristol Mercury*, 1 August 1846.
202   *Ibid*, 16 January 1847.
203   *Aberdare Times*, 2 September 1871.
204   *Swansea and Glamorgan Herald*, 10 April 1861.
205   *Shipping & Mercantile Gazette*, 29 September 1877.
206   *Taunton Courier and Western Advertiser*, 22 March; *Central Glamorgan Gazette*, 24 March 1871.
207   *North Devon Journal*, 3 June 1875.
208   Charles E. Lee, *The Swansea and Mumbles Railway*, Oakwood Press, 2nd. Edition, 9 & 13.
209   *Welshman*, 24 October 1851.
210   D. S. M. Barrie, *A Regional History of the Railways of Great Britain, Volume XII, South Wales*. (David St John Thomas, 2nd Edition, 1994), *passim*.
211   *Bristol Mercury*, 3 January 1852.
212   *Ibid*, 18 May 1867.
213   Poster in Author's Collection.
214   *Cambria Daily Leader*, 26 August 1861.
215   *Cardiff and Merthyr Guardian*, 28 January 1854.

Chapter 10

216 *Welshman*, 9 April 1847.
217 *Cardiff and Merthyr Guardian*, 10 April 1847.
218 *Monmouthshire Merlin*, 10 July 1847.
219 *Bristol Mercury*, 22 September 1855.
220 *Swansea and Glamorgan Herald*, 17 December 1862.
221 *Ibid*, 24 December 1862.
222 *Monmouthshire Merlin*, 17 January 1863.
223 *Western Daily Press*, 29 March 1867.
224 *Cardiff Times*, 16 October, & *Cambrian*, 22 October 1875.

Chapter 11

225 *Principality*, 15 September 1848.
226 *Welshman*, 21 May 1847 in which she was referred to as the *Scorpio*; *Cardiff & Merthyr Guardian*, 27 November 1847; Ince, 166.
227 *Shipping & Mercantile Gazette*, 22 November; *Welshman*, 28 November 1851.
228 *Bristol Mercury*, 29 November 1851.
229 *Bristol Times & Mirror*, 7 February 1852.
230 *Shipping & Mercantile Gazette*, 25 February 1852.
231 *Welshman*, 14 July 1854.
232 *Silurian*, 2 September 1854.
233 *Brecon County Times*, 29 August 1868.
234 *Central Glamorgan Gazette*, 5 May 1876.
235 *North Devon Journal*, 11 May 1876.
236 *Bristol Mercury & Western Daily Press*, 8 May 1886.
237 *Lloyd's List* & *South Wales Daily News*, 3 January 1878.
238 *Lloyd's List*, 24 March 1881.
239 *Ibid*, 20 September 1890.
240 WGAS D/D PRO/CA/S, Neath Abbey, 3948 (1869).
241 *Brecon County Times*, 13 February 1869.
242 *Cambria Daily Leader*, 9 February 1869.
243 *South Wales Daily News*, 22 May 1872.
244 WGAS D/D PRO/CA/S, Neath Abbey, 3948 (1871)
245 *North Devon Journal*, 16 August & *North Devon Advertiser*, 17 August 1877.
246 *South Wales Daily News*, 13 & 14 October 1885.

Chapter 12

247 *www.welshmariners.org.uk/n_contents.php?lang*
248 WGAS D/D PRO/CA/S, Neath Abbey, 3948 (1878 & 1879).
249 *Cambrian*, 1 May 1874. Also quoted by Paul Jenkins, *Twenty by Fourteen. A History of the South Wales Tinplate Industry*, (Gomer. 1995), 184.

250 Philip Bagwell, 'Salaries and Wages', in Simmons and Bidwell (eds.), *Oxford Companion to British Railway History*, (Oxford University Press, 1997,) 431–432.
251 *Bristol Mercury*, 1 August 1846.
252 *swanseamariners.org.uk/shipowners.php*
253 *Swansea & Glamorgan Herald*, 1 March & *Cardiff & Merthyr Guardian*, 4 March 1848.
254 *swanseamariners.org.uk/shipowners.php*
255 WGAS D/D PRO SR/S/1846/17/5 (Letter 1 Sept. 1847, from Collector & Comptroller, Customs, Bristol, to the Collector and Comptroller, Swansea.
256 *Central Glamorgan Gazette*, 2 June 1871.
257 *Ibid*, 22 December 1871.
258 *Ibid*, 14 March 1873.
259 *Weekly Mail*, 22 May 1880.
260 WGAS D/D PRO/SR/S/1846/17/3. Letter 6 August 1852 Collector & Controller, Customs, Bristol to Collector and Controller Swansea.
261 *www.swanseamariners.org.uk/shipsregister.php*
262 WGAS D/D PRO/CA/S, Neath Abbey, 3948 (1867). (*swanseamariners.org.uk* is incorrect.)
263 *Brecon County Times*, 4 January 1868.
264 WGAS Reference D/D PRO/CA/S, Neath Abbey, 3948 (1867).
265 *Cambria Daily Leader*, 11 April 1870.
266 *Star of Gwent*, 8 May 1875.
267 WGAS D/D PRO/CA/S, Neath Abbey, 3948 (1866 & 1867).
268 *North Devon Journal*, 20 May 1875.
269 WGAS D/D PRO/CA/S, Neath Abbey, 3948 (1881).
270 *Shipping & Mercantile Gazette*, 30 June 1882 and other dates.
271 *Western Daily Press*, 25 June 1906.
272 WGAS D/D PRO/CA/S, Neath Abbey, 3948 (1881).
273 Bristol Archives 30182/538 (Neath Abbey).
274 *Gloucester Citizen*, 12 November 1885.
275 *Western Daily Press*, 8 May 1886.
276 WGAS D/D PRO/CA/S Neath Abbey, 3948 (1881, 1882, 1883 & 1884; Bristol Reference 30182/538 (1886 & 1887).
277 Bristol Archives 30182/538 (Neath Abbey). Memorandum with List D for period January to June 1890 and List D for 1 Jan to 19 June 1894.
278 Bristol Archives 30182/538 (Neath Abbey).
279 *Ibid*, 30182/538 (Neath Abbey).
280 *Glamorgan Gazette* 29 June, 1894
281 WGAS D/D PRO/CA/S, Neath Abbey, 3948 (1866).
282 WGAS D/D PRO/CA/S, Neath Abbey, 3948 (1866 & 1867).
283 WGAS D/D PRO/CA/S, Neath Abbey, 3948, (1870).
284 *www.swanseamariners.org.uk/swanseamariners.php*

ENDNOTES

129

285 *Greenock Telegraph* and *Western Mail*, 10 July 1880.
286 *South Wales Daily News*, 17 July 1880.
287 WGAS   D/D PRO/CA/S, Neath Abbey, 3948 (1883).
288 WGAS   D/D PRO/CA/S, Neath Abbey, 3948 (1880).
289 WGAS   D/D PRO/CA/S, Neath Abbey, 3948 (1880 & 1881).
290 *Carmarthen Journal*, 3 December 1880.
291 WGAS   D/D PRO/CA/S, Neath Abbey, 3948 (1881).
292 *South Wales Daily News*, 14 October 1885.
293 Bristol Archives   30182/538 (Neath Abbey); *Glamorgan Gazette*, 29 June 1894.
294 WGAS   D/D PRO/CA/S, Neath Abbey, 3948 (1870).
295 WGAS   D/D PRO/CA/S, Neath Abbey, 3948 (1866, 1867, 1869, 1870, 1871, 1872, 1878 & 1879).
296 WGAS   D/D PRO/CA/S, Neath Abbey, 3948 (1872, 1873 & 1874).
297 WGAS   D/D PRO/CA/S, Neath Abbey, 3948 (1874).
298 WGAS   D/D PRO/CA/S, Neath Abbey, 3948 (1878, 1879 & 1880).
299 WGAS   D/D PRO/CA/S, Neath Abbey, 3948 (1880, 1881 & 1882).
300 WGAS   D/D PRO/CA/S, Neath Abbey, 3948 (1883, 1884).
301 Bristol Archives   30182/538 (Neath Abbey).
302 Bristol Archives   30182/538 (Neath Abbey).
303 WGAS   D/D PRO/CA/S, Neath Abbey, 3948 (1880, 1884).
304 Bristol Archives   30182/538 (Neath Abbey).
305 *Ibid.*
306 *Ibid.*
307 *Ibid.*
308 *Ibid.*
309 *Glamorgan Gazette*, 29 June 1894.
310 WGAS   D/D PRO/CA/S, Neath Abbey, 3948 (1867).
311 WGAS   D/D PRO/CA/S, Neath Abbey, 3948 (1871).
312 WGAS   D/D PRO/CA/S, Neath Abbey, 3948 (1879).
313 WGAS   D/D PRO/CA/S, Neath Abbey, 3948 (1866, 1867, 1869 & 1870).
314 *Western Daily Press*, 12 January 1863.
315 WGAS   D/D PRO/CA/S, Neath Abbey, 3948 (1872, 1873 & 1874).
316 *Cambrian News*, 11 February 1876.
317 WGAS   D/D PRO/CA/S, Neath Abbey, 3948 (1874, 1878, 1879 & 1880).
318 WGAS   D/D PRO/CA/S, Neath Abbey, 3948 (1880 & 1884).
319 Bristol Archives   30182/538 (Neath Abbey).
320 *Ibid.*
321 *Western Daily Press*, 22 June, *Cardiff Times*, 23 June 1894; Bristol Archives 30182/538 (Neath Abbey).
322 *Bristol Mercury*, 21 June 1894.

Chapter 13

323 John Morris, 'Evan Evans and the Vale of Neath Brewery,' *Morgannwg*, Vol. IX, (1965), 38–60 (51).
324 *Welshman*, 14 May 1847.
325 D. Rhys Phillips, 445–446.
326 *Welshman*, 9 April 1847.
327 *Monmouthshire Merlin*, 10 July 1847.
328 *Bristol Mercury*, 22 September 1847.
329 *Ibid*, 8 & 15 September 1855.
330 Green, 10.
331 WGAS   D/D PRO/SR/S/1871/2/7.
332 WGAS   D/D PRO/CA/S, Neath Abbey, 3948 (1880).
333 *North Wales Express*, 31 December 1880.
334 WGAS   D/D PRO/CA/S, Neath Abbey, 3948 (1880).
335 WGAS   D/D PRO/CA/S, Neath Abbey, 3948 (1882).
336 WGAS   D/D PRO/SR/S Neath Abbey, 3948 (1871)/8.
337 Copy of card provided by Carmarthenshire Archivist.
338 Bristol Archives   37908/1/12 (Neath Abbey).
339 *Lloyd's List*, 19 December and *Cambrian*, 23 December 1887.
340 *South Wales Daily News*, 28 January 1888.
341 *Bristol Mercury*, 22 January 1890, also *South Wales Daily News*.
342 *South Wales Daily News*, 18 & 29 April 1890.
343 Bristol Archives   37908/1/12 (Neath Abbey).
344 *Western Morning News*, 11 August 1894.

Chapter 14

345 *Shipping Gazette and Lloyd's List*, 19 December 1887.
346 *Bristol Mercury*, 21 June 1894.
347 *Ibid*, 1 August 1857.
348 *Slater's Directory of North & South Wales*, 1880, 241.
349 *Cardiff Shipping & Mercantile Gazette*, various dates 1884.
350 *Swansea and Glamorgan Herald*, 6 August; *Cambria Daily Leader*, 16 August 1890.

Chapter 15

351 *Bristol Mercury*, 1 August 1846 and later.
352 *Welshman*, 9 April 1847.
353 *Ibid*, 25 July 1851.
354 *Swansea and Glamorgan Herald*, 24 December 1862.
355 *Aberdare Times*, 2 September 1871.

356 R. P. Brereton, *Mr. Brereton's Report with Plan on the Floating of the River Neath. September 30, 1872*. (Whittington, Neath, 1872). (NAS).
357 Brereton's Plan.
358 O. S. Glamorgan Sheet XVI Surveyed: 1876 to 1877, Published: 1884 Accessed 9 Aug. 23.
359 D. Rhys Phillips, 313
360 Ince, 165.
361 *www.swanseamariners.org.uk/shipsregister.php*
362 *Hereford Journal*, 7 July 1847.
363 Green, 107.
364 *Welshman*, 25 July 1851.
365 *Swansea and Glamorgan Herald*, 12 September 1860.
366 *Cambria Daily Leader*, 10 January 1862.
367 *Swansea and Glamorgan Herald*, 6 April 1867.
368 *Morning Advertiser*, 15 November 1872.
369 *Swansea and Glamorgan Herald*, 24 December 1862.
370 *Central Glamorgan Gazette*, 29 July 1892.
371 *Swansea and Glamorgan Herald*, 10 April 1861.
372 Plan of Briton Ferry showing River Neath, Briton Ferry Docks, etc. c. 1860. NAS RE 13/8.

Chapter 16

373 John Newman, *Glamorgan*. (*The Buildings of Wales*, Yale University Press, 2004), 421.
374 *Glamorgan Gazette*, 29 June 1894, evidence given at the inquest by Richard Wilson, Principal Keeper of the Nash Lighthouse.
375 Bristol Archives 30182/538 (Neath Abbey).
376 *Lloyd's List*, 13 June 1894.
377 *Bristol Mercury*, 16 June 1894.
378 *South Wales Daily News*, 19 June 1894.
379 *Bristol Mercury*, 21 June 1894.
380 *Ibid*, 21 & 22 June 1894; *Glamorgan Gazette*, 29 June, 1894
381 Bristol Archives 37908 (Neath Abbey).
382 *South Wales Echo*, 20 June 1894.
383 *St. James's Gazette*, 21 June 1894.
384 *Bristol Mercury*, 21 June 1894.
385 *Western Daily Press*, 21 June 1894.
386 *Lloyd's List*, 22 June 1894.
387 *Coflein* NPRN273965.
388 *South Wales Echo*, 20 June 1894.
389 *Lloyd's List*, 2 July 1894.

390 *Glamorgan Gazette*, 29 June 1894.
391 *Western Mail* and other newspapers, 28 June 1894.
392 *Glamorgan Gazette*, 29 June 1894.
393 *South Wales Daily News*, 25 June 1894.
394 *Cambrian*, 29 June 1894.
395 *Ibid*, 6 July 1894.
396 *South Wales Daily News*, 28 June 1894.
397 *Lloyd's List*, 4 & 18 July 1894.

Chapter 17

398 From information provided by the Manager, Neath Port Authority.

Appendix 1

399 Various advertisements in *Bristol Mercury*, *Welshman*, *Cardiff and Merthyr Guardian* and *Swansea and Glamorgan Herald*.

Appendix 2

400 *Cardiff Times*, 4 August 1883.
401 *Swansea & Glamorgan Herald*, 29 June 1859.
402 *Cardiff Shipping & Mercantile Gazette*, various dates 1884.
403 *Butcher's Swansea & District Directory 1881-82*, 429.
404 *Brecon County Times*, 11 April 1868.
405 *Cardiff Times*, 9 January 1897.
406 *Brecon County Times*, 26 September 1868.
407 *Cambrian*, 29 March 1878.
408 *http://www.neathantiquariansociety.co.uk/news* Article by Peter Stevens 29 May 2017.
409 *Cambrian*, 4 March 1870; and *South Wales Daily Post*, 7 March 1893.
410 *Cambrian*, 21 September 1883.
411 *North Wales Express*, 31 December 1880.
412 Farr, 137.
413 *Cardiff Times*, 9 January 1897.
414 *South Wales Daily Post*, 8 January 1897.

Appendix 3

415 *Western Morning News*, 11 August 1894; *Cambrian*, 29 March 1895.
416 *Western Morning News*, 11 August 1894.
417 *South Wales Daily Post*, 28 March 1895.
418 *South Wales Daily Post*, 16 March 1898.

www.ingramcontent.com/pod-product-compliance
Lightning Source LLC
Chambersburg PA
CBHW042143160426
43201CB00022B/2386